DEPARTMENT OF EDUCATION AND SCIENCE

3.75

KU-518-129

SAFETY
IN OUTDOOR
EDUCATION

NEWMAN COLLEGE
BARTLEY GREEN
BIRMINGHAM, 32.

CLASS	371.775 363.147
ACCESSION	90719
AUTHOR	GRE

08

N 0004622 1

London: Her Majesty's Stationery Office

© Crown copyright 1989
First published 1989

ISBN 0 11 270690 8

CONTENTS

WITHDRAWN

PREFACE

This publication replaces the Department of Education and Science pamphlet, *Safety in Outdoor Pursuits*, first published in 1972. It has been written jointly with the Scottish Education Department, the Welsh Office Education Department and the Department of Education, Northern Ireland. The intention has been to draw on the best advice available. Acknowledgement is given to the many organisations and individuals who have participated in the process of consultation.

The scope of the advice has been broadened to cover recent developments in the use of the outdoors for educational purposes. It is also intended to encourage greater awareness of the educational value of learning out-of-doors and to emphasise that safety considerations should be appraised alongside a full consideration of the aims and objectives of any particular venture.

This publication is intended for all who have responsibility for providing activities and learning experiences out-of-doors and in residential centres for young people in schools, colleges, youth organisations and clubs. It refers to **providers** (those with legal responsibility for the conduct of activities, such as local education authorities and governing bodies), **co-ordinators** (those who plan outdoor education in individual institutions or organisations), **leaders** (those in overall charge of activities), and **instructors** (those in immediate control of an activity out-of-doors). Everyone in these categories, including voluntary instructors, has a duty to take reasonable care for the safety of young people who may be affected by what they do.

Under statute and common law, responsibility for safety in maintained establishments rests mainly with local education authorities; in independent establishments it rests with governing bodies or proprietors; and in voluntary youth organisations with the governing council.

While every effort has been made to give the best advice available, no claim is made for comprehensiveness, nor should the contents be taken as giving an authoritative interpretation of the law.

This publication should be read in association with other documents which contain advice complementary to that given here. Some are listed in Appendix 11. Others may be recommended by responsible authorities.

SAFE

PRACTICE
IN OUTDOOR
EDUCATION

Safe practice in outdoor education

Introduction Traditionally the term 'outdoor education' has been applied to activities out-of doors which involve some degree of physical challenge and risk. The focus wa often on the skills of particular outdoor pursuits and on developing confidence to manage in hazardous environments. Such activities still have their place but the concept of outdoor education has widened.

A range of visits, journeys, expeditions on land and water and airborne activities either for part of a day or for a longer period, is now used as a means of makin many aspects of school and college work more profitable for young people. Such visits, especially those which have a residential element, play an important part in promoting the personal and social development of young people as well a contributing to their understanding of particular subjects and topics.

Sometimes the focus of activities out-of-doors will be on the process by which young people learn and this will have implications for the role of both the leade and the participants. Experiences may be more self-directed and young people will learn from the process of planning, discovery and reflection rather than from the directed activity prescribed by the leaders. In these circumstances it is harde to set down precise regulations about safety. Leaders will need to consider the size and make-up of the group, the aims of the activity and the chosen environment, as well as the needs of individuals in terms of their persona development in such areas as relationships, self-esteem, self-confidence and competence.

Outdoor education, with its emphasis on the skills and challenge of living travelling and learning out-of-doors, has close affinities with environmenta education which seeks to make young people aware of their environment and to develop their knowledge and understanding of it. Fieldwork in town and country i an essential part of outdoor education. Often, but not always, this will be enhanced by an element of adventure and may involve some physical challenge Practical enquiry-based learning out-of-doors is an important element of study in many subject areas and in new courses and examinations.

Outdoor education provides opportunities for learning through experience and direct investigation of the many features and phenomena to be found out-of doors. These present young people with practical problems such as finding route, crossing a stream, keeping warm and dry and having due regard for safety Exploration in towns and in the countryside is often a good starting-point for developing awareness and concern for both familiar and unfamiliar aspects of the environment. However, young people should not only gain knowledge about places they visit, but they should also develop responsible attitudes toward them, to others who use them and to those who live and work there.

The duty of care enshrined in the principle of being *in loco parentis* should not be undertaken lightly for once assumed it cannot be set aside until the young people are returned to the care of their parents. Those who undertake this responsibility must be prepared to exercise the control which this role requires.

Principles of safety

- The quality of **leadership** is vital (see **Leadership** below). Experience and sound judgement are the most important constituents; when appropriate they should be reinforced by a nationally recognised training scheme and by a qualification or by locally relevant training. The ratio of instructors to participants should be in keeping with the ability and experience of the group and the conditions to be encountered. In hazardous outdoor environments a duty of extra care is required of leaders in order to protect the physical and psychological health of the young people.

- The nomination of a person in each institution and organisation with responsibility for off-site activities and journeys – the **co-ordinator** – can do much to ensure that programmes are conducted safely, that common procedures are adopted and that relevant training is provided for the staff involved.

- There is no short cut to the acquisition of **skill, physical fitness and knowledge** by the leaders and group members. Progressive and continuous training is a vital feature of any programme. Competence and confidence need to be developed over time.

- The quality of personal and group **equipment** should conform to the standards recommended by responsible national agencies. Some items of clothing and equipment may be designed and made by the young people themselves. Many courses now encourage this and include designing and making outdoor clothing as a valuable part of the programme.

- The **procedures** for the conduct of any expedition should be made known to parents, organisers and all participants.

- **Awareness of danger** and potential hazards is developed through experience (see **Leadership** below). Leaders need to be able to anticipate the possible risks involved in using particular environments, in engaging in certain fieldwork activities, or in using different types of transport. Risks will be minimised if leaders are familiar with members of their groups, their strengths, weaknesses, personalities and previous experience. The visit, journey or expedition needs to be matched to the ages, ability and experience of participants.

- **Weather conditions** can dramatically influence the activity; seasonal changes in temperature, wind strength or the amount of rain, snow or cloud cover can rapidly alter the nature of a locality. Fortunately, weather forecasts are readily available through television, radio, the press and by telephone, but leaders should err on the side of caution in interpreting them (see **Inconsistent weather**, p.21).

- **A list of members** of the party should be carried and these need to be supported by a regular count of members of the group. Supervision is usually more effective if groups are small and accompanied by a designated leader,

3

rather than a large group under the control of several leaders.
● Irresponsible behaviour can be a threat to the safety of the group, the leaders and the public. A **vigilant approach** is required by group leaders to ensure that responsible and appropriate standards of behaviour are maintained at all times.

Preventive action The importance of preventive strategies, as advocated by the Water and Leisure Department of the Royal Society for the Prevention of Accidents (RoSPA)[1], cannot be over-emphasised. Intervention before participants get into difficulties is essential. Safe practice is dependent upon:
● awareness of potential hazards and dangers;
● sound judgement of what constitutes a dangerous situation;
● preventing access to dangerous situations for those ill-equipped to cope;
● adequate supervision; and
● knowledge of how to help oneself and others in danger.

Leaders are urged to adopt this preventive approach. In many accidents a contributory factor has been the lack of control or discipline which may become more difficult to maintain in an outdoor environment. Responsibilities rest here not only with leaders but also with parents and the young people themselves.

Reporting injuries Under the Reporting of Injuries and Dangerous Occurrences Regulations (SI.1985/2033 or the Scottish or Northern Ireland equivalent), all serious injuries to employed persons, pupils, trainees and students must be reported to the Health and Safety Executive. The analysis of returns is providing an indication of the pattern and incidence of accidents from which policies for their prevention are being developed.

Leadership Competent leadership is the most important safety factor of all. Special training and experience are essential for all who take parties of young people on expeditions into potentially hazardous environments; enthusiasm in itself is not enough. Leaders need to be able to safeguard the physical and psychological health of the young people in their care. They should limit their activities to those where they have specialised knowledge or skills. (For leadership training in land activities see **Leadership training**, p.18.) There are national and local awards in outdoor pursuits and others that provide evidence of leadership skills in the outdoors. These are useful qualifications for those who take young people into open country, on to water or into the air. Leaders or instructors may also be qualified by relevant and recent experience.

In-service training There is a need to establish progressive in-service training which will provide leaders with experience on completion that is appropriate to their needs. To achieve this, it is important for authorities to have specialist advice available and to provide guidelines on qualifications and procedures required for training and

1. Addresses of organisations mentioned in the text are shown in Appendix 11.

expedition planning. Procedures should be established for vetting and giving approval for expeditions into hazardous areas and for providing the necessary network of appropriate specialist advice. Some local authorities have designed their own training programmes to meet the specific needs of teachers operating in particular environments. Many outdoor education activities involve young people in low-risk initiative or problem-solving activities which require little technical skill on the part of the leader but a clear understanding of educational aims, imagination and sound leadership qualities.

Staffing ratios Most authorities provide guidelines on staffing ratios, especially in relation to hazardous activities, which naturally vary according to the activity, its location and the experience of the group. Nevertheless, it is important to emphasise that these prescribed staffing ratios are for guidance and do not remove from the provider, co-ordinator or leader the duty to ensure that the group is adequately staffed throughout a particular visit. For example, there are particular hazards associated with fieldwork visits to beaches and leaders will need to exercise close supervision and observation to take account of varying tides and weather conditions. Similarly, guidance is needed on the different circumstances applying for primary age pupils and those with special educational needs.

Communication Group control and communication outside the group is an essential feature of good practice. In activities on land a system for recalling the members of a group together is necessary whenever a party may become scattered. A list of members of the party should be carried by the leader and another left at base so that an immediate check may be made of group members in the event of an emergency. Expedition plans and proposed routes should also be available at base and where necessary there should be arrangements for reporting back at intervals on the progress of the party.

Learning to Challenge and adventure are never free of risk. Learning to have regard for the
assess risk safety and welfare of oneself and others is an aspect of personal development of participants to which outdoor education can make an important contribution. However, there must always be an acceptable framework of safety. It is indefensible to expose young people to dangerous conditions and unnecessary risks. The co-ordinator and the responsible authority should ensure that there is appropriate leadership and proper planning and administration of educational visits and journeys.

An essential outcome of any outdoor activity programme is the ability to recognise danger and to understand how, by forethought and preparation, it can be minimised if not eliminated. On occasions, hazards may appear to young people to be greater than they really are, and an extra challenge may be derived from facing up to them when the leader is confident that no real danger exists. Similarly, young people may be unaware of the dangers that exist. Nevertheless, the appreciation of hazards and the need for confidence and common sense in countering them must be emphasised from the start. If activities are chosen to match the age and experience of young people, the participants are able to become involved with the leader in assessing possible hazards and deciding on appropriate responses for themselves. For example, young people could be involved in considering the insulating properties of dry versus wet clothing, the effects of extreme cold, the need for adequate food and drink, the planning and following of a route, or the signs and effects of exhaustion.

Self-reliance Self-reliance and self-awareness are often important aims of outdoor education. Therefore expeditions and activities should not only meet safety requirements but they should also provide opportunities for young people to be involved in planning and decision-making. The Duke of Edinburgh's Award Scheme, for example encourages young people to be independent and self-reliant in planning and carrying out expeditions by land or water following appropriate training. The skills, knowledge and attitudes needed before groups are able to work independently will depend on their training, the nature of the activity and the environment. Training of a progressive nature will be necessary and a careful assessment needs to be made of the competence of individuals. The self-reliance of individuals can be increased gradually but careful consideration should be given by the instructor to deteriorating conditions or emergency situations.

Giving responsibility progressively to young people so that they learn from their successes and mistakes requires experience and judgement on the part of the leader. Small groups are the best medium for such learning, so that leadership develops and changes according to circumstances. As confidence develops young people need time in which to explore areas and activities without close supervision. More adventurous expeditions can be the culmination of such training leading to opportunities for developing self-reliance and initiative. Many young people gain in confidence and performance by being physically and emotionally stretched up to, but not beyond, reasonable limits.

Review of activity An important element of outdoor or residential experience is the review. Discussion of what has happened should occur informally at the time or in a structured way. It should assist participants to see the significance of what has been achieved and learned. The process might begin with individuals recalling for themselves the events that have occurred and could be developed by analysis in groups. The process of review might lead to decisions about future programmes and intentions. The whole process of planning, experience, structured review and personal reflection needs to involve young people at each stage. Review sessions contribute a great deal to the value of outdoor and residential experience, and staff training in the skills and methods of conducting review sessions is a valuable aid to good practice. Handled inappropriately, a review could be damaging to the confidence or self-esteem of participants.

Safety guidelines from organisations It is important that those responsible for organised parties should be familiar with the safety and legal guidelines that exist. Many local authorities, independent schools and voluntary organisations have prepared their own regulations and booklets of advice specific to certain areas and circumstances (see Appendix 11). Many adopt a system for the notification and approval of school visits and journeys (see Appendix 1). Guidelines on safety must emphasise that safe conduct is never an 'extra' consideration, but an integral part of each activity and, however elementary, affords opportunity for the encouragement of personal responsibility. Many education authorities have recently carried out reviews of policy statements, which hitherto had dealt only with safety advice. In consultation with advisers and centre staff, they have identified a rationale for outdoor education together with aims, objectives, content, methodology and methods of evaluation. Reviews have taken account of the wide variety of settings in which activities take place. They stress that responsibilities for the conduct of school visits and journeys and the procedures for reporting, recording and reviewing accidents or hazardous incidents should be defined. The preparation of local codes and safety guidelines is strongly recommended.

Insurance Co-ordinators responsible for managing groups should clarify with their authority what insurance provision is already made and what additional insurance will need to be taken out. In some cases the costs of insurance may be delegated as part of a statutory scheme of local management of schools, and advice should be obtained from the relevant source. Special arrangements will be necessary to obtain insurance cover for activities abroad. Advice on insurance cover is difficult to give here since practice varies and standard policies are not always sufficiently comprehensive. It is therefore wise to check whether the policy covers:
- public liability of the responsible authority covering claims for negligence
- third-party liability covering claims against the responsible authority and its employees
- personal accident cover for leaders, voluntary helpers and party members
- medical treatment
- transport and passenger liability
- high risk activities (often excluded from standard policies)
- damage to or loss of personal or hired equipment
- curricular as well as extra-curricular activities
- transport and accommodation expenses in case of emergency
- compensation against cancellation or delay
- compensation for loss of baggage and effects
- third-party risks when using vehicles within the EC and other countries
- legal assistance in the recovery of claims
- failure or bankruptcy of the travel company

Leaders should scrutinise carefully the list of exclusions in their policy, particularly where overseas travel is planned.

Safe practice in outdoor education

Keeping parents, governors and responsible officers informed

Parents and governors of schools are now expected to be involved in planning activities away from the school site. They should be fully informed of the kind of activities contemplated. Information should be supplied to parents at an early stage in the planning so that they can make their decision on a properly informed basis and before being committed financially. Parents' prior consent to their child's participation and to emergency medical treatment should be obtained in writing. Full information should be provided about the activities to be undertaken, the staff involved and arrangements for supervision. Leaders should inform themselves of the general fitness and health of all members of the party. It is a great advantage in this respect if school medical records are up to date.

Where young people are to be away overnight or for a longer period, parents should be able to meet the accompanying staff and volunteer helpers concerned. This will mean that consent is given on an informed basis. A record should be kept of any questions and answers provided at such a meeting with parents. Parents must evaluate the information provided and reach their own decisions about supporting the venture. Once committed, parents and young people have a duty to support the activity by ensuring reasonable behaviour and co-operation with leaders. Parents need to be informed of occasions when young people will not be directly supervised.

A meeting of staff and parents should be planned to cover the following:
- the aims and objectives of the visit, journey, activity or expedition
- its duration
- a code of conduct
- mode of travel and the name of any travel company to be used
- a precise statement of insurance cover
- activities planned, including any that are hazardous, with some indication of a typical daily programme
- the parents' responsibility for ensuring that young people are fit to participate
- clothing requirements
- times when participants will not be directly supervised
- luggage, type and labelling
- the base or bases from which the group will be operating
- the place and time of the start and the return, particularly if either of these is away from the home base or outside normal session times
- other arrangements for picking up and dispersal of the group
- if the journey is an extended one, some reassurance that there will be effective communication links between the leader, co-ordinator and the operating authority in case an emergency should arise
- financial matters.

A draft parental consent form is shown in Appendix 2 and this may be considered for use by providers and co-ordinators. Three copies of the form are desirable one for the parent to keep, one for the head of the institution and one for the group leader. A standard parental consent form should be included in any general information booklet distributed to parents.

Charging for school activities The charging provisions of the Education Reform Act apply from 1 April 1989. After that date, charging is permitted for certain strictly defined school activities, mainly those which are optional and take place outside school hours.

DES Circular 2/89, sent to all LEAs and schools in January 1989, explains that the legislation resulted from a number of successful challenges to existing charging practices and pressure from many quarters for the law to be clarified. The provisions in the 1988 Act:
• maintain the right to free school education by forbidding charges for any activities which take place in school time, with the exception of individual tuition in a musical instrument
• give LEAs and schools discretion to charge for activities provided wholly or mainly outside school hours, as long as these activities are optional extras and are not required to meet the school's statutory curriculum obligations, nor to complete the syllabus for a prescribed public examination
• permit charges for board and lodging provided for pupils on residential courses
• require LEAs and schools to draw up statements of their policies on charging and to say in what circumstances they might exempt some parents from charges. As a legal minimum, parents receiving income support or family credit should be exempted from board and lodging charges where a residential activity is classified for the purposes of the legislation as taking place in school hours, or is otherwise an essential part of the curriculum provided for the pupil
• remind schools that although charging is forbidden for school-time activities, they can still invite parents and others to make voluntary contributions towards school funds or in support of any specific project. If a particular activity is dependent upon voluntary contributions for its survival, this can be explained to parents at the early planning stage, although it must also be clear that if the activity goes ahead no pupil will be left out because his or her parents have not contributed towards the cost.

Expeditions Expedition work is a normal outcome of camping, canoeing, climbing, caving, sailing and skiing activities in schools, youth clubs and colleges. In good conditions an expedition in open or mountainous country or on water appears deceptively simple and safe. The dangers are not always obvious and may not become apparent until some time after a wrong decision has been taken. Without knowledgeable leadership and the right equipment and clothing an unpleasant experience can turn into tragedy. It is disturbing that serious accidents have occurred because those responsible have not taken sufficient account of the

Safe practice in outdoor education

considerable knowledge and advice which is available locally, or from operating authorities and training agencies.

For the Duke of Edinburgh's Award Scheme training and assessment expeditions in wild country areas, the Wild Country Expedition Panel should be notified of the route, timing and composition of the group. Notification is made to Panel Secretaries, whose names and addresses are available from the Duke of Edinburgh's Award Scheme office (see Appendix 11).

Organisation and planning

Important elements of any successful expedition on land, water or in the air are meticulous planning and organisation, including study of the weather pattern of the area and of recent forecasts. Planning is also essential for safety. Participants should be involved in the task of preparation; this is the best way of engendering positive attitudes toward safety.

The following points are intended to serve as guidelines. Emphasis will vary according to individual requirements, in particular, the duration of the expedition the experience of the group and level of supervision to be applied.
- Once the aim of an expedition is clear, there is no substitute for first-hand **knowledge of the area**. Normally, at least one person in authority, preferably the leader, should be familiar with the district and the local conditions likely to be encountered. In certain circumstances, the aim may be to explore a little known area or stretch of water. In such a case a well qualified or experienced leader should be able to assess the terrain and plan accordingly.
- The factors governing the choice of **equipment and clothing** should be determined early. Financial considerations may be important, but the type of environment, climatic conditions, the degree of mobility necessary, and the available transport should be the major factors in selecting equipment.
- The group should be adequately prepared for an expedition. **Training programmes** should include a thorough course in the techniques and skills of safe movement in open country, on water or in the air and in the management of equipment. This will not only inspire individual confidence but also will help to develop a corporate spirit. (See also **Principles of safety**, p.3, and Appendix 9.)

Residential visits and journeys

Many groups are based either at education authority (LEA) centres or at suitable centres provided by youth or commercial organisations. Residential courses where young people live and work together provide valuable learning opportunities and an exciting environment, but safety factors must not be ignored. The way in which authorities exercise their responsibility for educational visits and journeys varies according to the nature and type of visit or activity to be undertaken.

Although the legal implications are well known, it is important to emphasise that the teacher or leader in charge of a group is *in loco parentis* throughout the residential period, and that the head or co-ordinator, whether accompanying the group or not, also has a responsibility for ensuring appropriate supervision and planning. This applies equally to non-residential visits. School governors in England, Wales and Northern Ireland have responsibility for the general direction and conduct of the curriculum of the school and this includes extra-curricular activities such as visits and journeys. They also have statutory responsibilities on health and safety, the scope of which will increase with the introduction of local management of schools. In Scotland, the responsibility rests with education authorities. Apart from safety aspects, the responsible authorities will wish to be satisfied about the aims and objectives of such visits and journeys and about the implications for pupils remaining in school if the visit is in term time.

Residential centres
Many educational visits based at residential centres will include plans for outdoor activities and the centre's safety rules relevant to each of these activities should be strictly followed. Most authorities insist that those responsible should hold specific qualifications and it is vital that staff and participants are comprehensively prepared and briefed for the activities to be undertaken. Such preparations should also cover residential aspects, including an assessment of the suitability of the accommodation, facilities and the qualification of staff to provide instruction in particular activities. The centre should never be left unattended by staff when it is being used by young people.

In staffed residential centres, the overall responsibility for the direction and management of courses is usually vested in the principal or head of the centre who, in turn, delegates to members of the residential team. Each day, a duty member of staff is appointed to deal with routine matters and respond to any emergencies. Visiting staff are asked to share responsibility for the smooth running of courses and for the pastoral care, behaviour and discipline of pupils; they are asked to accompany groups and share the learning experiences but are seldom required to undertake sole responsibility for leading groups during adventurous pursuits. The organisational role of the visiting teacher needs to be identified in advance. Often more could be made of their expertise and knowledge of the needs of the group members. This could be achieved by involving them in planning with staff at the centre. Some centres are used on a self-programming basis without supervision and in these circumstances it becomes even more necessary to have prior visits and careful planning.

Personal rights and discipline
Planning and organisation should be such that young people are not exposed to risk of racial, sexual or physical abuse or harassment by adults or others within a peer group, either when taking part in an outdoor activity or when in a residential setting.

The law now requires all adults who have significant contact with young people under 18 to disclose any convictions of a criminal nature to the organising authority. Reference should be made to DES Circular 12/88 (HOC 102/88) *Protection of Children: Disclosure of criminal background of those with access to children,* available from the Home Office. There is a specimen form of applicatio for a police check to be made. Operating authorities may have their own detaile guidance.

Good discipline is essential to the success and safety of any visit. Codes c conduct in relation to smoking, alcohol and behaviour between the sexes need t be clearly established and understood.

Leaders also need to be aware of the symptoms and dangers associated wit alcohol, drug and solvent abuse.

Urban fieldwork

Many outdoor activities take place in towns and cities which can be mor dangerous than expeditions and pursuits in wild country. Young people should nc participate in an urban fieldwork exercise unless the leader has visited the wor area beforehand and, ideally, explored it. There may well be all sorts of potentia hazards which need cause no danger given careful forethought. Road junctions railway lines, canals and disused buildings are some examples of dangers tha pupils must be warned of beforehand. Young people also need to be warne about how they approach strangers, both individuals and groups, especially i lonely areas or in environments with which they are unfamiliar.

Leaders need to ensure that each participant involved in urban fieldwork is abl to follow clear instructions on where to go, where to return to and what to do late or in an emergency. Ideally, the safest arrangement is for young people t work together in small groups. This will allow for effective supervision and reduce the chances of individuals becoming separated. Young people should be c sufficient age and ability before being left unsupervised and should be left for onl short periods in the first instance, with regular checks being made.

Visits abroad   Most authorities place visits abroad in a separate category in framing thei regulations. They require groups to seek approval from the responsible authority and to provide more detail than is required for other visits and journeys.

A journey abroad calls for detailed thought and planning and the services of reputable tour operator experienced in group travel can be a great advantage.

There may be medical requirements imposed by the country to be visited.

Because of language difficulties it may be helpful for all members of the party t carry the address and telephone number of the hotel or hostel in case a individual is separated.

An essential practice for journeys abroad is to require leaders to submit names c participants to the authority in advance. This considerably assists in the event o an emergency when there is no one available at the home base. It shoul however be a requirement for all visits and journeys that in the event of ar emergency a contact be available at or near the home base known to botl parents and the responsible authority. Where a participant is injured, authorities normally have reporting procedures which must be followed.

Fire safety Dormitories and corridors in residential accommodation often present young people with a new and confusing experience. It is well known that people in unfamiliar surroundings, possibly in another country, will easily become confused and disorientated especially when an emergency arises. A responsible adult should ensure that a set of clearly defined duties for action in an emergency is available and that those to whom the duties have been allocated understand them and have experience in performing them.

These duties should include ensuring that:
- all exit routes from dormitories and other sleeping accommodation are clearly indicated;
- the posted instructions are clear and have been read to new visitors and are understood;
- smoking is prohibited in the dormitories;
- a leader of responsible age is appointed to each dormitory and possesses a reliable torch where emergency lighting is not provided;
- a fire drill is held during the first day for new visitors;
- where the centre does not have a clear and published policy on fire routine the responsible adult should be required to formulate one on arrival;
- the arrangements for calling the fire brigade are adequate and understood and that someone has the duty to make such a call on hearing the alarm where there is no member of the permanent staff already holding this duty;
- the person should be made aware of the full address of the building/camp to ensure prompt response by the fire brigade, as well as the location of the nearest telephones;
- all occupants are familiar with emergency procedures and escape routes.

A fire safety checklist is given in Appendix 4.

First aid Leaders should have a working knowledge of first aid. Small accidents sometimes happen during outdoor activities and the actions of those around at the time can greatly affect the eventual outcome. It is therefore as well for all staff involved to possess an understanding of how to cope with the most common slight injuries and to develop an awareness of appropriate courses of action in emergencies. On all activities, the leader should carry a first aid pack appropriate to the planned activity and all staff should be aware of its contents and how they should be used. Leaders of more advanced activities or those operating in remote areas will need to consider whether they are appropriately qualified and equipped to deal with emergencies.

First aid regulations cover all employees, both teaching and non-teaching staff. Although pupils and students are not covered by these regulations, employers, such as local education authorities, boards of governors or proprietors, have legal duty of care.

Every educational institution or organisation should have suitably equipped firs aid boxes in easily accessible places. Portable first aid kits should be available t groups taking part in outside activities. Staff responsible for first aid should chec first aid packs and carry out regular inventories of the contents to ensure tha adequate supplies of each item are available.

Attention is drawn to the advice concerning Acquired Immune Deficienc Syndrome (AIDS) given in the publications listed in Appendix 11. No cases ar recorded of Human Immunodeficiency Virus (HIV) infection having bee transmitted as a result of direct mouth-to-mouth resuscitation, although there is theoretical risk where there are cuts or sores in the mouth. In an emergency direct mouth-to-mouth resuscitation should not therefore be withheld. 'Rigi airway' mouthpieces for resuscitation may be used only by first aiders who hav had special training in their use.

Road safety On average over 1,800 pedestrians, including some 260 children, are killed on th roads every year, representing a third of all road deaths. Many more are injurec Traffic is a hazard all young people have to cope with and it is essential that the and their leaders have a good working knowledge of road safety matters, and ar familiar with the rules of the Highway Code. Precautions are as necessary in th country as in the city. Cars may be travelling faster on country roads an pavements may be narrow or non-existent.

The Green Cross Code is a good guide for all pedestrians, and it is important tha children are taught how to follow it. When out walking groups should use th pavements and paths provided. Two adults are needed for the smallest group c young people, one to be at the front and one at the back of the group. Gaps in th line should be avoided and there should be frequent stops to check that all is wel Young people should be briefed at the start on the aims and direction of the walk If there is no footpath parties should walk in single file on the right hand side c the road facing oncoming traffic. Walkers should carry something light coloure or bright and wear something reflective in the dark. A group of people marchin in formation on the road should keep to the left, with lookouts in the front an back wearing reflective clothing at night and fluorescent clothing by day. At nigh the front lookout should carry a white light and the back one a bright red light Leaders must beware of other road users and follow the Highway Code. For visit abroad the differences in traffic regulations should be clearly explained t members of the party.

Use of minibuses Most authorities issue separate regulations concerning the use of minibuses These regulations should be observed as part of the preparation for a visit o journey and proper maintenance checks carried out.

Attention is drawn to the Transport Act, 1985 (Sections 18–23). (See Department of Transport address, Appendix 11.) This new legislation governs the conditions under which education and welfare bodies are exempt from public service vehicle (PSV) licensing when using vehicles adapted to carry 8–16 passengers, even if they are carrying them for 'hire or reward'; they operate instead under the authority of a permit issued under the Act. (In Northern Ireland, under the Road Traffic (NI) Order 1981, there is no such exemption.) Drivers have to be over 21 years of age and have a full driving licence (not provisional) and the vehicle must meet prescribed conditions of fitness which incorporate the key safety provisions of PSV regulations. The responsible authority should ensure that drivers have appropriate experience. Special care is necessary when towing boats or trailers.

The current Department of Transport booklet *Public Service Vehicles 385* (available from Room S17/03, 2 Marsham Street, London SW1P 3EB) describing the operation of the relevant sections of the Act should be consulted. When using a minibus abroad, it is essential to check the regulations concerning the use of a tachograph in any vehicle adapted to carry eight or more passengers. Details are contained in another Department of Transport booklet *Public Service Vehicles 375* (available from Room S16/04, 2 Marsham Street, London SW1P 3EB).

Care of the environment Matters of environmental care and conservation should, like safely, be considered at each stage of outdoor education. An awareness of and regard for the principles of conservation need to be fostered continually by the leader. Most organisations and groups provide preparation and briefing for visits to centres, and this usually emphasises the need for considerate behaviour, adherence to the Country Code and other codes for fieldwork, the removal of litter, consideration when using rivers, lakes or the sea, the preservation of flora and fauna and the prevention of footpath erosion. Camping demands special care in leaving sites clean and free of litter and ensuring that the camp makes minimum impact on the area. Some groups take even more positive action by including a period of service to the local community as part of the programme for a centre visit. Where possible, this should be encouraged. Further advice on the care of the environment is available from organisations listed in Appendix 11.

Field studies There has been considerable growth in the number of field study excursions associated with course work, especially in geography, biology and geology. Such excursions include farm and industrial visits, urban fieldwork, ecological studies, hydrological and geomorphological fieldwork and geological investigations at sites such as quarries. All these activities require vigilant and effective supervision at all times.

Leaders should know that legal protection is afforded to certain plants and animals under the Wildlife and Countryside Act 1981.

Safe practice in outdoor education

The scope of field studies is such that leaders of groups need to be adequate trained, prepared and properly equipped for the particular activities the undertake. This is particularly so where field studies take place in wild hazardous environments.

It is also desirable that leaders should attend a course designed to raise the awareness of safety issues and the many other problems that can arise durir field excursions. This might include topics such as emergency procedures in th event of an accident, first aid, awareness of the hazards of the environmen importance of knowledge of weather conditions and the general responsibilitie of party leadership.

Educational visits to farms are becoming increasingly common and a particularly valuable for young people from an urban environment. Many farm offer ancillary activities such as nature trails or forest walks. Specific guidance c safety when visiting a farm should be obtained. Particular hazards are associate with tractors, grain or slurry pits, chemicals, and farm animals which may k easily frightened.

Further sources of advice on the conduct of field studies and visits are included Appendix 11.

Visits to national parks
All those concerned with the organisation of visits to the national parks in Englan and Wales should make the fullest possible use of the service which the nation. parks Youth and Schools Liaison Officers can provide. They offer not only detaile local knowledge of the area and advice on safety and access and on loc weather conditions, but also considerable expertise, information and resource which are useful to teachers and youth leaders. Countryside ranger services Scotland and Northern Ireland provide similar advice and guidance on resource for educational visits. Current relevant addresses are listed in Appendix 10. view of the heavy use made by school and youth parties of certain sites national parks and areas of outstanding beauty or scientific interest, it necessary to be fully aware of ways to minimise the impact on them by groups.

SAFETY

ON LAND

Safety on land

Introduction Interest in the countryside is ever-increasing and the network of footpaths, b ways and bridleways in this country offers a unique opportunity to young peop to explore and learn about their environment whilst taking physical recreatic There is a wealth of published material relating to routes through the countrysi available to co-ordinators and leaders which would be extremely valuable planning and executing such activities. The Countryside Commission a Ramblers' Association are good points of contact for advice. A checklist f **safety on land** is given in Appendix 6.

Leadership training The new Basic Expedition Training Award (BETA) of the Central Council of Physic Recreation (CCPR) is a national qualification for leaders involved in fieldwork a accompanying groups in the urban fringes, green fields and low hills. The traini for the award lasts at least 90 hours followed by 30 hours' supervised volunta service when skills acquired can be developed. Training emphasises leadersh organisational skills and effective decision-making. The Duke of Edinburgh Award Scheme has considerable experience of providing expeditions for you people and has available well illustrated and authoritative guidance for leade Information and help is also provided by the Young Explorers' Trust and t Expedition Advisory Centre (see Appendix 11).

Problem solving/ initiative exercises There is an increasing use of wild and open country environments for proble solving and initiative exercises, some of which make use of elements of mc traditional activities, such as the ability to use ropes to safeguard moveme Such activities require experienced and competent leadership including a cle understanding of educational aims, specific objectives and imagination, as well a knowledge of water safety, personal protective clothing and equipment. Whe appropriate, leaders should also be thoroughly familiar with any special skills requirements relating to the technical use of potentially hazardous environmen Much of the value of such exercises is in allowing groups and individuals to lea from their mistakes. The ability to assess when intervention is necessary (perha on the grounds of safety) is an essential quality of leaders in these activities.

Potential hazards The main hazards in the field are indicated below.

Hypothermia Exposure of the body to progressive cooling as a result of particular weath conditions and loss of body heat, accompanied by a progressive deterioration body condition, is known as hypothermia. Hypothermia can occur at any time the year on hills. Factors that contribute to this are often a combination anxiety, unfitness, damp, cold, wind and over-exertion. Sometimes it is broug about by inadequate waterproofing or insulation leading to excessive loss of he or energy. The victim may have experienced a recent illness, or had poor sleep inadequate food. In extreme cases hypothermia rapidly results in death unle symptoms are recognised quickly and immediate preventive action is take

18

The symptoms are:
- a slowing down of pace or effort – though this sometimes alternates with unexpected bursts of energy
- shivering and tiredness
- aggressive response to advice
- abnormality of vision, and stumbling
- slurring of speech.

Individually, or in any combination, all these are indications of the onset of hypothermia. If the victim is either urged to greater effort or left unprotected, the consequences can be serious.

The most effective action is to stop where the best shelter from the wind can be gained and to insulate the casualty against further heat loss until help arrives. Additional clothing, sleeping bags or survival bags, even over wet garments, can help. Energy foods and hot drinks are beneficial and, should breathing stop, mouth-to-mouth resuscitation is vital (see **First aid,** p.13). Suitable protective clothing, a carefully planned route which includes escape routes, adequate training for young people and attention to local weather forecasts can all help to reduce the dangers of exposure. By careful observation and by monitoring performance and weather conditions many dangers can be anticipated and a decision made to descend to more sheltered country or return to base. It is equally important to be on the lookout for other physiological effects on individuals such as frost nip, heat exhaustion or sunburn.

Losing the way   Navigational and map-reading errors can lead to unforeseen changes of route. These may expose a party to highly dangerous situations. The best safeguard is therefore skilled leadership and prior knowledge of the terrain. The leader will need to take decisions in the light of prevailing circumstances. Whenever possible, a list of members of the party and an expedition route card with a brief outline of the route proposed should be left at base, or with a responsible person if the base is unmanned. Route cards left at base giving details of compass bearings and estimated times of arrival at intermediate and terminal points are particularly important. Emergency routes should be decided upon before leaving and alternative routes to be followed in the event of bad weather should be recorded on the card. If in emergency an alternative route has been taken, contact with the base should be made as soon as possible.

The following standard procedures should be considered by both leaders and members of a party for use when lost:
- The leader should **keep the group together**, remain calm and assess the fitness of the party in the conditions prevailing.
- The leader should find out if possible from the map the approximate **location** of the party and consider the best escape route.
- If mist prevents the position being fixed, an attempt to **descend** below the

mist level should be made. Descent should be by an easy route and should not be hurried. It may be necessary to protect a member of the party with an emergency rope as the party progresses. When clear visibility is reached, the precise location of the party should be established and the route revised if necessary.

● If darkness is approaching, or a member of the group is exhausted and cannot continue, **preparation for a night out** may have to be made. This is a extremely serious step and should only be considered if descent is not possible too hazardous. The party should be settled as comfortably as possible using both natural shelter and emergency food and equipment. In very cold weather everyone should exercise arms and legs frequently and take care that nothing restricting the circulation of blood; for example, boot laces should be slackened In these circumstances, the leader must be capable of keeping the spirit of the group high and should make regular checks to ensure that each member protected from the elements.

● If there is sufficient experience within the group and weather condition permit, leaders should consider **sending for help**, though they need to be aware of the dangers of splitting the party.

● The party should know and use the **International Alpine Distress Signal** (six blasts on a whistle, or flashes of a torch, or movements to attract attention, with minute between each pattern) to guide a possible rescue party. They should also know a rescue party's standard response to the distress call (three signals within the minute, followed by one minute's pause).

● When the party has reached safety, the leader should at once send **confirmation to base**, to the original destination and to the police.

Retreat from potential danger   A decision to turn back is often difficult to take but it is wiser than placing a party in a position of risk. Retreat should be by means of the easiest walking route Skill in rope handling on steep ground may be vital to the safety of the party, and an emergency rope may therefore be necessary. A party should try to remain together unless there has been an accident, although with a trained assistant leader splitting up can be contemplated.

Rivers in spate   A few hours of heavy rain can make river crossing dangerous, particularly Scotland, and it should be avoided except in an emergency; it is wiser to make even a long detour to use a bridge. Rivers in spate which are knee depth or above should not be crossed. If a crossing is unavoidable, techniques should be employed to lessen the risk of being swept away. (Details are given in publications listed in Appendix 11.) Leaders should be aware that some members may be distressed from exposure after crossing. It is always best to avoid routes which include crossing even small streams as these may quickly swell in conditions thawing snow or heavy rain.

Contaminated food or water   Prevention is better than cure. The general health of the party and strict routine for sanitation are of the utmost importance. Water from a doubtful source should always be boiled or sterilised by tablets before use for drinking or cooking. Procedures for the safe handling, storage and cooking of food should be made known (see **Campcraft**, p.27), as should the hazards of eating plants found in the wild.

Inconsistent weather   Hills in Great Britain and Northern Ireland are noted for the inconsistency of their weather. In remote areas help is less accessible. An expedition to Wales or the Lake District in April or May is likely to experience very different conditions from those in Scotland where winter conditions usually cover the period from November to May. The dangers associated with rapid changes in the weather, which often bring conditions of extreme cold, should never be underestimated. The weather forecast should be obtained by means of television, radio, newspapers, telephone weather forecasts, local weather centres, and experienced local advice.

Weather forecasts are available by contacting the following:
National 24-hour weather forecasts service 0898 500 400
National forecast for five days ahead and further details 0890 500 430
'Mountaincall' – weather forecast for the Scottish Highlands 0898 500 442

The leader should be aware of the weather forecast and its implications for the safety of the party. Changes in weather should be monitored, as rapid changes are a serious threat to the safety of a party in mountainous country.

Loose rocks   Leaders should avoid areas of loose rocks when moving on cliffs or scree slopes or in gullies. If such areas must be used, leaders should be familiar with methods of negotiating such terrain. Careful route selection and positioning of the party are essential.

Fear   In unfamiliar situations, especially where there is an element of risk, some people easily take fright. An understanding but prompt and reassuring approach is necessary, since even a single affected person can put a party at risk.

Mountain walking *Leaders*   Leaders holding one of the national Mountainwalking Leader Training Certificates or Awards will have technical competence to conduct parties in mountainous or remote country. Leaders should be encouraged to take this training or a locally based scheme designed for moorland areas such as the Pennines. Responsible authorities should satisfy themselves that those in charge of young people have been suitably trained and have the necessary skills and experience to operate in particular environments. (See **Leadership training**, p.18.)

Prior to 1979 the Mountain Leadership Certificate was administered by the British Mountaineering Council (BMC). Subsequently, the certificate has been replaced by an award issued by the English Mountainwalking Leader Training Board which, through its log book, reflects the skills and experience of the holder. Similar schemes are administered by the Scottish Mountain Leader Training Board

Safety on land

(SMLTB), Welsh Mountain Leader Training Board and the Northern Irela Mountain Training Board. The SMLTB also administers national summer a winter awards for those who lead others walking in the hills and mountains whe the use of ropes is not envisaged. The Mountaineering Instructors' Certifica (MIC) is jointly administered by the BMC and SMLTB for those who wish to tea basic mountaineering techniques in summer and winter.

Walking skills Training in mountain walking skills must include the accurate judgement of pac mastery of the rhythm and balance necessary to safe movement, and t conservation of energy. Except in an emergency a party should keep together; one should be allowed to straggle behind because, apart from the danger, it c also intensify feelings of exhaustion and depression. Running downhill can dangerous in certain terrain. When descending a scree slope, a group should so positioned that loose stones dislodged in movement do not prove a hazard others.

Winter conditions The leader's responsibilities are demanding and only a skilful and experienc leader should attempt to lead parties into the hills in wintry conditions. Even th it is advisable to keep to lower routes where emergency action can be mc readily taken. The possession of the SMLTB Winter Certificate is appropriate leaders accompanying groups to the Scottish mountains and the higl mountains of England and Wales where the weather conditions can often severe. Where winter climbing is envisaged, the MIC is the relevant qualification.

Being on mountains in winter demands fitness, stamina and determinatic Severe conditions call for very efficient waterproof and windproof clothing (s Appendix 9). Navigation is difficult in snow conditions, travel is slower and enen consuming, and movement requires judgement, backed up by skill and reserv of strength. The danger of becoming stranded overnight is greater in winter a no leader should expose a group of young people to such a risk. Late starts a often a prime cause of such situations.

Practice in the use of an ice axe and crampons should initially be carried out easy terrain with safe run outs. From the outset young people should be taug the basic method of arresting a fall. The greatest care must be exercised wh walking on snow or over ice-covered streams or rivers. When moving near ridg and heads of gullies care must be taken to avoid cornices, which could bre away several feet from the edge. Experience is essential in the use of a rope a in fixing snow and ice belays in cases where dangerous areas of snow and have to be negotiated. If it seems likely that to go on means prolonged a extensive use of the rope, the party should retrace its steps and move off t mountain.

In severe winter conditions parties should be aware of the dangers of avalanc and should recognise the importance of obtaining specialist local advice prior setting out on mountaineering journeys. This knowledge should include an awareness of weather history which is essential to identify the likely risk of avalanche on the slopes. The leader should know when it is safe to glissade. For inexperienced young people this is a dangerous practice and should not be encouraged since a slide can very quickly get out of control and end in disaster. Some modern fabrics have little friction and allow the body to accelerate in a slide. Sliding should never be allowed unless the leader has made sure that there is a clear run out at the bottom of the slope where it is possible to come to rest without harm, and that the slope is free of boulders and rocks.

Rock-climbing Rock-climbing with young people should be introduced in easy stages. No one should be over extended until the basic skills and procedures are understood. Where appropriate, beginners should be given experience of holding another climber on a rope and of being held themselves. A safety rope should be used in abseiling practice and gloves worn. Approved protective helmets should be worn. The nature of the tuition and teaching ratios for this activity will depend on the level and purpose of the session and the experience of the participants.

Leaders Some local training schemes have been devised for approving leaders using accessible single pitch outcrops. The British Mountaineering Council (BMC) is presently producing *Guidance notes for single pitch rock-climbing supervisors*, which offer advice on safe techniques of rock-climbing and cover aspects of good practice including group management and organisation, conservation and access, and ethics of the sport.

It is essential for party leaders to be familiar with rope management and the skills of moving through rocky terrain. Leaders will need to ensure adequate and appropriate guidance and supervision. They must be able to appreciate the limitations of their climbing group on steep rocks, to assess the potential dangers of difficult terrain and be able to give competent aid in rescue and emergency. Experience of basic rock-climbing should include the ability to abseil, to select sound belays and to lead in descent and ascent on easy rock. Training in the use of knots, and practice of the recognised calls and signals required for communication, can be covered indoors.

Ropes The BMC also offers authoritative advice on the selection and care of ropes and suitable knots for particular purposes. Simple precautions to keep ropes in good condition, and points to look for when considering replacement, are clearly set out. It is necessary to keep a careful record of the age and use made of the ropes and to discard any which show signs of undue wear.

Climbing walls While there is no substitute for training and experience at the rock face, the recent development of artificial climbing walls offers new opportunities for teaching and practice. Such facilities should be carefully designed. Rock-climbing walls should only be used under the leadership of those with appropriate

Safety on land

experience. A handbook on the construction and use of climbing walls published jointly by the BMC and the Sports Council and should be consulted.

Skiing Where skiing takes place at recognised centres in the United Kingdom ar abroad and under qualified instructors, appropriate training and skilled obse vation of individual progress is usually assured. The leader of a visiting par should establish adequate liaison with the local instructors and ensure that the activities are consistent with the educational objectives. Leaders should mak sure that the members of the party are familiar with the local as well as th general skiing precautions and routines. Despite the presence of prepared piste lifts and restaurants, ski slopes can be hazardous environments for the unwary.

Leaders It is desirable that leaders should have received appropriate training or t accredited through a local leaders' course. These courses are run by the Englis Ski Council and the Scottish National Ski Council and cover all aspects of th organisation of school and youth group ski courses. Leaders who wish to instru their own pupils are advised to qualify as a coach, ski leader or ski instructor. A leaders should know how to summon the ski or piste patrol and carry a first aid k at all times.

Preparation Skiing, particularly for the beginner, is one of the most physically demandir sports. It requires a high level of endurance, strength and mobility, and a cours of fitness training prior to the visit is recommended. Some schools now hav access to an artificial ski slope. If possible, the group leader should organis lessons under the direction of a qualified instructor prior to the visit to the resor This is particularly beneficial to beginners as it familiarises them with th equipment and the basic techniques. Party leaders should also ensure th members get adequate sleep and food during the visit so that they are able t maintain the high energy expenditure required. It is essential that programme are carefully planned and adequately supervised to provide purposeful ar profitable activities off the slopes.

Behaviour Ski courses may use hotels where there are other guests who may be on holida Irresponsible behaviour can be a threat to safety. A vigilant approach is require by group leaders to ensure that responsible and appropriate standards behaviour are maintained. Special care is needed when visiting countries whe alcoholic drinks are easily available so that acceptable standards of conduct ar safety are maintained both on and off the ski slopes.

Equipment and The ski equipment supplied to groups booking through tour operators is norma
clothing of an acceptable standard. The length of the skis supplied will depend on th views of the local ski school but should not exceed the skier's own height. Sk must be fitted with adjustable release bindings and ski brakes. It is strong recommended that the bindings are checked for correct functioning on issu monitored in use and returned to the place of hire if bindings are incorrect

adjusted. The mechanism of the release bindings should be checked daily for fit and function and any difficulties reported immediately to the hire source.

It is essential that all skiers wear a ski suit consisting of jacket and salopettes which are wind- and snow-proof. Long-legged underwear (preferably not nylon which does not absorb perspiration and can cause blisters around the feet) should be worn when it is particularly cold. Gloves or mitts, a hat and ski boots which give support to the ankles are necessary. Better insulation results from wearing three or four layers of comparatively thin clothing rather than one or two thicker ones.

Exposure to bright sunlight on snow-covered slopes can cause severe sunburn and eyestrain. Skiers should use a screening cream on exposed skin and wear dark goggles or good sunglasses with plastic lenses, rather than glass lenses which are likely to splinter on impact. When skiing in Scotland, eye protection is extremely important because of the arduous weather conditions.

Ski instruction It would be ideal for each group to be accompanied by its own instructor holding the appropriate governing body award. It is usual, however, for ski courses to hire ski instructors at the local ski area. This can be done through the tour operators who are increasingly using instructors qualified by the British Association of Ski Instructors, whose address is given in Appendix 11. When arranging for ski instruction, consideration should be given to the age and ability of the group. The hours of instruction will vary accordingly.

Skiers' code Accidents will be reduced if the following precautions are observed:
- No pupils are allowed to ski alone or outside marked skiing areas and trails.
- Supervised skiing practice and other snow activities are carefully monitored.
- Clear instructions are given to pupils about the runs, tows and chairlifts to be used, about check-in and return times and about rendezvous points and safety procedures.

Nordic skiing This activity is rapidly growing in popularity as it can be carried out with relatively little snow on level terrain. However, it is an energetic activity in winter conditions and there are a number of factors to be taken into consideration. Leaders who wish to instruct their own groups should seek the qualification of the British Association of Ski Instructors (Nordic) or a local equivalent in order to acquire instructional expertise leading to safe and progressive skill development on suitable terrain. While the activity can be conducted in areas away from hills, there is a tendency to seek snow on higher ground when it is absent on lower slopes. This increases the potential risk and the need for further qualified and experienced leadership.

Ski mountaineering Ski mountaineering, whether using standard or Nordic equipment, is potentially hazardous because of factors such as the remoteness of the terrain, deep snow, the risk of avalanche, problems over route finding, and the steepness of the terrain. Considerations must be given to the leader's skill and experience and th ability of the group before this form of skiing is undertaken. Appropriate trainir and qualifications are available through national governing bodies and nation mountain centres.

Information When skiing in Scotland, weather and snow information can be obtained t telephone from the Scottish Meteorological Office.

Caving Before being introduced to caving young people should ideally have son experience of other activities making similar physical demands. Many caves c not provide a suitable environment in which to introduce people to strenuoι activity; conditions are often hostile and they could result in exhaustion ε exposure. The National Caving Association Training Committee exists to improν the recreational caver's awareness of all aspects of the underground environme and, in particular, the technical skills and knowledge necessary to explore cavε and potholes with optimum safety and comfort. The Committee also endeavou to promote high standards of leadership in those taking parties underground.

Leaders A leader must be an experienced caver. In 1983 the Cave Instructor Certifica (CIC) and the Local Cave Leader Assessment (LCLA) Schemes were establishe The syllabus for the CIC Scheme and a core syllabus for the LCLA Schemes a available from the Secretary of the Training Committee in the docume *Leadership and Instructor Qualifications in Caving.* The CIC Scheme designed for those involved in introducing others to caving, passing technic skills on to others and instructing in a variety of caves throughout Britain different technical levels. The LCLA Scheme provides suitable guidance ar certification for local leaders.

On no account should the leader take beginners into a cave system which wοι tax his or her own ability. In deciding the size of a party the leader must take in account the degree of difficulty of the system. The exploration of a cave is group activity. The group should be small, both for mobility underground and ε that each person is able to be an integral member of the group. As far as possib each member of the party should be self-reliant at the level of the difficul attempted. If the cave system demands a reduction in numbers the party shou consist of at least four people. The reactions of individual members to unfamilι situations should be carefully noted by the leader and anyone whose behaviour attitude might put the party at risk should be excluded.

Equipment and The basic personal equipment for each caver should include a warm ar
clothing protective outer garment, stout boots (without hook lacing if laddering), protective helmet with chin strap and lamp bracket, and an efficient headlamp torch. Emergency rations and lighting spares should be carried by the grou Leaders should carry a whistle and a first aid kit. Wet suits, ladders and oth equipment will be taken as required to meet the conditions of the trip.

Precautions Protective clothing and safety equipment must be checked. Details of the passages to be followed should be left at base and leaders should leave some indication of their presence at the entrance to the cave system being explored. The leader must be satisfied that there is a wide margin of safety in case of heavy rain while the party is in the cave. The leader and the assistant (who brings up the rear) should have clear lines of communication to keep a check on the condition of the party and to allow a decision to be made to turn back in the event of a mishap. A life-line should be used when there is danger of a fall and when ascending and descending pitches.

Surface training should include practice in climbing a ladder in caving gear. Ladders must have life-lines which should be held by experienced and competent cavers.

Mines All mines, including slate, lead, copper and other mineral mines, should be treated with the greatest caution. Only working mines that are properly maintained and open to the public can be regarded as safe. Disused mines can deteriorate quickly as materials used for access or support rot or rust away. In the exploration of disused mines there is always a danger of broken and falling rock and collapsing tunnels from former blasting. Parties should never be taken into coal mines unless they are open to the public and are approved by British Coal.

Radon gas Scientists have drawn attention to the possibility of high radiation levels in certain cave systems due to a concentration of radon gas. The risk, where it exists, is to those who use the caves frequently and regularly, such as instructors. Detailed advice may be obtained from the Health and Safety Executive (Mine and Quarry Inspectorate) and the National Radiological Protection Board.

Campcraft The value of camping as an educational activity is widely recognised. Through camping, young people learn to live comfortably and efficiently out-of-doors, to accept and value personal qualities of behaviour and to develop interests in the natural environment. (See **Care of the environment,** p.15.) In general, efficient camping is safe camping. Nevertheless, accidents cannot always be prevented, however careful the planning and thorough the precautions. On standing camps the most common accidents are caused through the wrong or careless use of tools or through misadventure in the fire or cooking areas. There may also be hazards in the immediate environment of the camp of which all should be made aware (see **Potential hazards,** p.18).

The skills of campcraft are vital to the safety and success of many expeditions.

Tents In the choice and preparation of the site, it is wise to expect the worst possible weather and every precaution should be taken to ensure that the party stays secure and dry under all conditions. Tents should be pitched to allow free movement between them and to prevent risk of fire spreading. The ability to live

safely and comfortably with no more canvas or equipment than can be carried t
a team on foot requires a high degree of competence, skill and preparation.

Choice of tent and techniques of siting and pitching under all conditions requii
considerable practice and experience. Tents vary greatly in quality and desig
and careful selection is necessary to ensure stability and protection in the wor:
conditions. In mountains it is advisable to have a tent with a sewn-in ground-shee
and a down-to-earth fly-sheet giving protection all round. Good ventilation
essential to reduce condensation and to prevent danger from fumes if cookir
has to be done inside a tent doorway. Teamwork, skill and experience will affe
the conditions of living in a tent. Systematic procedures concerned wit
sanitation, the organisation of food and equipment and economy of movement
a tent will all contribute towards acceptable standards of safety and hygiene.

Catering   Catering skills and satisfactory diet are important factors in the maintenance
morale and general fitness. Weight, cost, acceptability and simplicity
preparation need to be considered in selecting food-stuffs, and knowledge
dehydrated foods may be valuable. Flexible planning is essential since weath
conditions often dictate changes in the menu. Parties should always car
emergency packs of food which, if wrapped correctly and undamaged, will kee
for long periods, though they should be checked before each expedition. Eatir
small quantities of energy-giving foods during the day is beneficial and
especially advisable in adverse conditions.

Each tent party should be able to cook as a self-contained unit, although in mi
conditions group cooking is often more efficient. Cooking equipment and foc
should be apportioned to cater for the separate needs of each tent or pair
tents. Cooking in a tent doorway calls for a high level of competence and
minimum of movement.

The safe handling of stoves in all conditions should be practised. Stoves ar
utensils should always be made stable. Great care should be taken whe
exchanging butane cylinders or refilling pressure stoves. If alcohol burners a
used specific advice should be given. In particular, burners should be cool befo
any attempt is made to refill them. These operations should never be carried o
in or near the tent or near a naked flame. All groups should be trained and t
familiar with the characteristics and potential hazards of different types of stove
No flammable materials should be stored near the cooking area and there shou
be adequate first aid facilities on site.

Hazards   Hazards in the immediate environment of a camp are often less predictable tha
those met en route to a site. A leader must indicate clearly to the party und
what conditions groups may explore the surrounding area in their leisure tim
Unaccompanied parties should not be less than four in number. The leader shou
be confident that they will act responsibly and remain together when outside th

camp boundaries. It is also advisable to take a roll call each time the party moves off, at meal times and each night before retiring. Leaders should know the location of the nearest telephone, casualty hospital and doctor. Special care should be taken about bathing or swimming (see **Swimming**, p.35).

Horse-riding Riding schools recognised by the British Horse Society will provide high standards of instruction for young people. A list of approved establishments appears in the annual directory *Where to Ride*. A pamphlet, *Ride More Safely*, which deals with all aspects of road safety with horses, can be obtained from the British Horse Society. Suitable clothing should be worn, and basic essentials are hats of the current BSI standard and footwear with low, hard heels. Trainers or wellingtons are not suitable.

Pony-trekking Pony-trekking and trail riding have become increasingly popular activities with school and youth groups and often involve movement over hilly and scenic terrain. But pony-trekking may involve long hours in the saddle and some preliminary riding instruction is advisable. Weather conditions and terrain may make it necessary for protective clothing to be worn.

Routes liable to weather hazards, such as unexpected fog or slippery conditions following heavy rain, should not be taken except on reliable local advice. The Highway Code also contains suitable advice for riders on the road; this advice should be stringently observed.

Small groups are desirable for this activity and they should normally be accompanied by two adults with the overall leader holding at least the Assistant Instructors' Award of the British Horse Society.

Organisers of groups planning to use riding or trekking centres should ensure that the centre has a licence issued by the local authority under current legislation.

Orienteering Orienteering is not especially hazardous, but it is an all-year-round activity and accidents may occur in places where medical attention is not immediately available. It is desirable that teachers and others taking groups of young people to organised orienteering events should themselves have had some first-hand experience of the sport.

Competitive orienteering is one of the outdoor activities in which a young person may be entirely alone in the woodland or the countryside. In these circumstances there may be a very slight but possible risk of abuse or molestation which needs to be recognised and understood. In educational settings, young people should operate in pairs, especially in the introductory stages.

Equipment and clothing Much basic orienteering takes place in open country. However, when running through dense or abrasive undergrowth participants in orienteering events should have full leg and arm cover to minimise the risk of scratches and grazes which could lead to infection. Although events are not normally held in exposed areas,

Safety on land

competitors' clothing should give adequate protection against cold, wind and rain Stout footwear which will grip on sloping or slippery surfaces should be worn Every competitor must carry a whistle and know how to use it to summon assistance in the case of injury, either to themselves or to another competitor Leaders should warn groups against the frivolous use of whistles. A polythene map bag is essential and it is sensible for beginners to carry a watch.

Participation Those in charge of parties at organised events should ensure that eac competitor chooses a course which is appropriate to his/her age, fitness an previous experience. Leaders should ensure that beginners are aware of the scal and main symbols used on orienteering maps. It is particularly important to drav attention to areas marked 'out of bounds' and to the colour convention of th maps; open areas are yellow and wooded areas are shown as white or green.

Leaders should stress the importance of reporting to the finish and of handing i control cards. This requirement applies to all competitors whether they complet a course or retire. The matching of control cards to stubs handed in at the stai enables organisers to check at the conclusion of an event whether anyone is le in the competition area; if cards and stubs do not tally then a comprehensiv search is organised. Absolute beginners should be allowed to go in pairs if the wish and should be instructed to report to the finish after a set time, even if the have not completed the course. They should also be given clear instructior about what to do if they become lost.

If someone is apparently lost at the conclusion of such an activity, the person i charge should first check that the young person is missing and if so searc obvious features such as control points, paths or rides and boundaries. Othe participants should not be used to help in the search. It is then a matter c judgement, depending on the time of day and prevailing weather conditions, as t when the police should be alerted. It is a useful safety strategy to set an outsic time limit by which all participants must return to base.

Leaders Although young people may gain experience of orienteering through participatic in organised events, many teachers and youth leaders will wish to organise the own navigational activities. They should be fully aware of the coaching awar scheme and the safety recommendations of the British Orienteering Federatio Teachers and leaders wishing to develop the sport are advised to attend a instructors' award course organised by the Federation and to read the publicatic *Teaching Orienteering* which is obtainable from the governing body.

Terrain It is often feasible for activities to be based on a permanent orienteering course the locality. Failing this, the event organiser should endeavour to use a small are with clearly defined boundaries and take care to ensure that obvious hazare such as quarries, crags, deep ponds or marshes, major roads and railway lines a clearly marked 'out of bounds' on the map and, if necessary, taped off. Th planned duration and technical difficulty of the course should be well within the capabilities of the participants, and should involve safety strategies to limit the effects of navigational errors.

Rope courses and zip wires The safety rules should be relevant to the type of activity concerned, taking into account the general height, degree of difficulty, risk of fall, type of ground below and obstacles. The aim of the rules must be to preserve life and limb and to ensure that however great the apparent danger the actual risk is negligible. Adequate precautions, such as the provision of a soft landing area, should be taken to safeguard users. Suitable clothing should be worn, and attention should be drawn to the potential dangers of wearing jewellery and having long hair that is not tied back or covered. Great care must be taken when there is an element of competition and leaders need to ensure that no undue pressure is put on young people to complete the course or activity or to race against time.

Aerial runways are probably the most dangerous of the many 'off the ground' activities undertaken by young people and serious accidents can result from their misuse. Even when all reasonable precautions both in construction and use have been taken, an element of hazard will remain. The aim, therefore, should be to eliminate all avoidable risks and to exercise the highest degree of responsibility in their use.

Construction Structures should always be 'fail safe', and before a runway is constructed the precise purpose, nature of use and potential hazards need to be carefully considered. Considerable experience in construction is required and the materials used are often critical for safety. Metal hawsers and natural fibres should not normally be mixed on the same structure because of the differences in breaking strain. Permanent structures should be subject to regular inspection for signs of deterioration and wear and a record of these inspections maintained. Participants should be protected by safety lines at all times and there should always be sufficient staff available to be able to observe the pupil on the runway as well as to supervise others. The Scout Association has prepared useful guidelines, the *Aerial Runway Code*, which should be studied carefully before constructing and using a runway.

Cycling Cycling is a popular activity for young people, but the increase in traffic even on minor roads means that vigilance is necessary. Every care must be taken by leaders to ensure that youngsters understand correct behaviour and are aware of likely dangers en route. Before allowing young people on the roads, leaders must be sure that participants are proficient cyclists and know the Highway Code. On quiet roads it will usually be safe to cycle two abreast, but if there is traffic on the road it will be necessary to proceed in single file. If there are two leaders present, the best system of supervision is for one to be at the front of the party and the other at the rear. Ideally, groups should be no larger than ten, but if there are more participants, riding in two or more smaller groups a few minutes apart

31

should be considered. The pace of the group should always be comfortable fo the slowest participant.

Condition of bicycles Whether cycles are hired or belong to those taking part, they should be checke for roadworthiness and safety and be suitable to the size and weight of th participants. It is essential to check brakes, tyres and lights.

Touring Sound planning and preparation is required for cycle touring. The British Cyclin Federation and the Cyclists' Touring Club offer useful advice on such matters a choice of basic equipment, the loading and gearing of bikes, route planning an daily schedules. Many youngsters plan their own cycle tours and manage wel with advice and encouragement from parents, school or club.

Mountain and cross-country cycling Mountain and cross-country cycling, using specially designed and built cycles, i steadily increasing in popularity as a means of exploring the countryside. It is physically demanding sport that requires similar stamina and safety techniques t that necessary for mountain and hill walking. Groups should be small. Planne activities should be well within the capabilities of those taking part and leader need to ensure that any environmental damage and erosion are kept to minimum. Groups cycling in open country should show the utmost consideratio for other users of the countryside.

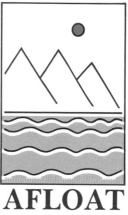

SAFETY

AFLOAT

Safety afloat

Introduction The use of water-borne and water-based activities for both educational and recreational purposes is increasing. Educational activity now takes a variety of forms. It may concentrate on the acquisition of physical skills, contribute to programmes of personal development, or add an additional dimension to the study of the environment. It is important that an individual's introduction to these activities emphasises the importance of safe practice, proper procedures, adequate training and the need for vigilance. Providers must always be aware of their responsibilities in these respects without diminishing the pleasure and the freedom which can accompany the activity. (A checklist for **safety afloat** is given in Appendix 7.)

In the development of outdoor education programmes the traditional water-borne activities of canoeing and sailing with their established safety codes have been complemented by a wide range of water-related activities such as wind surfing, fishing, sub-aqua swimming, raft-building, rubber-boating and gorge and river-walking. A number of safety principles are common to all water-related activities including:

- conducting the activity in suitable conditions;
- using appropriately qualified and experienced leaders;
- using appropriate and reliable equipment;
- subjecting equipment to regular and rigorous safety checks;
- ensuring participants have the level of water confidence needed for the activity.

Water confidence and swimming Water confidence is an important factor in all water-related activities. Depending on the activity, such confidence will be required near, on or in the water. Instilling and developing this confidence is an important aspect of outdoor education. All water-related activities will be enhanced if participants have their water confidence developed to the level needed for safe and enjoyable participation. This should be a prime objective for all providers.

Rescue training Appropriate instruction in water safety prior to participation in water-related activities is essential. Some appreciation of the differences between indoor and outdoor swimming environments is necessary, as is some awareness of the ability range of participants when swimming in open water. Training in safe swimming (including self-rescue), rescue and resuscitation is desirable. It is recommended that at least one leader should be competent in water rescue and life-saving techniques. The importance of a preventive strategy, however, cannot be over emphasised and the programme of activities should be organised with this in mind. (See **Preventive action**, p.4.)

Cold water immersion Despite extensive training in survival and life-saving techniques, cold water immersion, as the Royal Life Saving Society (RLSS) points out in its handbook

34

Resuscitation and First Aid, is a major contributory factor in drowning fatalities in the United Kingdom. Sudden entry into cold water can produce uncontrollable gasping, the end result of which can be dizziness or even loss of consciousness. Blood pressure and pulse rate can rise, the effects of which may be more serious for older participants or those with heart or circulatory disease. In very cold water (around 5°C) even strong swimmers are unlikely to keep afloat for more than a few minutes. Prolonged immersion will inevitably contribute to the onset of hypothermia, although the exact rate of heat loss will be dependent upon water temperature, amount of body fat, type of clothing and the amount of physical movement.

Providers should note that younger participants are more at risk because of the lack of body fat. It is important, therefore, that the need for adequate clothing for activities in which immersion in cold water is a possibility is stressed. Unnecessary movement in the water should be discouraged in order to reduce heat loss. Survival times are estimated by RoSPA to be considerably increased if casualties can float motionless with legs together and elbows to the sides. Providers should also emphasise the danger of drinking alcohol when engaged in water-related activities. Alcohol consumption, according to statistics analysed by RoSPA, is a contributory factor in approximately 25 per cent of all drownings

Personal buoyancy and clothing   Personal buoyancy aids or lifejackets, appropriate to the activity and conforming to the standards specified by the relevant governing body, should be worn by everyone engaged in the activity. Such aids should be of appropriate size and correctly worn and it is the responsibility of the leader of the activity to ensure that this is so. Regular and frequent testing of this equipment is essential to ensure that it is functioning properly. Providers should ensure that all participants have clothing and footwear suitable for the activity.

Swimming   Occasionally providers of outdoor education programmes will wish to offer swimming in the sea, lakes and rivers as an extension to the programme or for recreation. The conditions in which this activity is conducted will vary considerably, but great care in supervision is always required. Providers are urged to adopt the preventive strategy advocated in the section on **Preventive action** (p.4), and to be aware of the effects of sudden immersion in cold water.

Outdoor swimming for all its enjoyment is a hazardous activity. Local knowledge can be vitally important and awareness of tides, currents, cold, weeds, polluted water and unstable river or sea beds is essential. Particular care is needed when it is not possible to see the bottom or judge the depth of the water. Local sources of knowledge should be checked and it should be remembered that the absence of warning signs or markers does not guarantee safety. Participants should be clearly briefed regarding the limits of the swimming area. Supervision should be undertaken by persons capable of making a rescue and carrying out resuscitation. Supervisory training should not be neglected and should be designed to increase

Safety afloat

awareness of the risks inherent in the activity. The importance of encouraging responsible behaviour on the part of the participants should also be stressed within the staff training programme as should the need to control access to the activity.

Co-ordinators should be encouraged to produce written operating procedures which cover the conduct of outdoor swimming. The location of emergency equipment and a clearly understood alarm system should also be identified in these guidelines. Co-ordinators should also appreciate the importance of drawing up an appropriate emergency action plan.

Contaminated water Attention is drawn to the risks to health from contact with fresh water contaminated by the urine of domestic and wild animals or by the tissues of infected animals. Haemorrhagic Jaundice (Leptospirosis or Weil's Disease) is a recreational hazard to bathers, campers or sportspeople in infected areas. The illness has many manifestations which range from influenza-like symptoms to fatal disease. Rats and other rodents act as carrier hosts for the disease. Good hygiene practice is recommended. Scratches and abrasions should be covered with waterproof plaster before entering the water; inhalation or swallowing of water should be avoided and showers should be taken after fresh-water sports and other outdoor activities, particularly following immersion. In case of emergency reference should be made to the Leptospirosis Reference Unit Public Health Authority, County Hospital, Hereford HR1 2ER (telephone 0432 277707).

Canals Outdoor education programmes often make use of canals, particularly for water borne journeys. In addition to following the principles of safe practice referred to in the earlier paragraphs of this section, providers should be aware that canals pose a particular set of problems, especially for the unfamiliar user. Manoeuvring space for craft is often limited and tunnels and swing bridges may present difficulties. The use of locks requires special boat-handling skills if dangers are to be kept to a minimum and those involved must be adequately briefed and supervised by knowledgeable leaders. Advice and information about the use of canals, restrictions and closure for maintenance should be sought from the nearest office of the British Waterways Board.

Canoeing Canoeing offers considerable opportunities for developing a spirit of adventure for acquiring the skills of handling a small craft and for exploring new environments. There is, as in many outdoor activities, an inherent element of risk which can be minimised by taking reasonable precautions. Developing the water confidence of beginners is important because of the attendant dangers of capsize. It is necessary to exercise common sense and consideration for others at all times.

Planning The value of expeditions by canoe as a means of enhancing physical skills and personal and social development has long been recognised. The preparation for

36

such an activity should emphasise the need for a heightened awareness of safety. The planning should take account of the capabilities of the participants and should draw on the local knowledge available. Groups expeditioning in remote areas should be aware of special factors such as distance from emergency services and weather conditions. The current operational guidelines of the British Canoe Union (BCU), the Scottish Canoe Association (SCA) and the Canoe Association of Northern Ireland (CANI), and any subsequent revisions, should be followed.

Planning and preparation are crucial. The leader should ensure that the equipment selected is suitable for the conditions likely to be encountered and, if necessary, seek specialist advice. Participants should wear adequate clothing, if necessary wetsuits to prevent hypothermia, and, where appropriate, protective headgear. Local knowledge of the canoeing venue and operating conditions is invaluable and all providers are encouraged to obtain it when working away from their usual areas.

Care should be taken to select water appropriate to the level of expertise of the participants and leaders. Instructors should be aware of the dangers associated with locks, weirs, white water, overhanging trees, underwater obstructions and strong currents. There are particular dangers of infection associated with a capsize in stagnant or polluted water, for example. Access to water in England and Wales should be sought through the owners and in conjunction with the BCU. It should be noted that there are differences in Scotland and Northern Ireland in relation to the law and access to water. If further information is required the SCA or CANI should be contacted.

Leaders Providers are recommended to ensure that leaders and instructors supervising the activity are suitably experienced and, ideally, hold the appropriate qualification of the BCU, the SCA or CANI. Designated assistants should be competent canoeists. The BCU recommends supervision ratios of 1:8 for initial training in sheltered water and 1:6 on running or tidal water. The leader may, however, exercise discretion in adjusting ratios according to prevailing conditions and the experience of the group. Local training schemes operate for some canals and sheltered water where staffing ratios and procedures are determined by the prevailing conditions. Staffing ratios may need to be adjusted in certain circumstances, for example, when canoeing with special needs groups or groups with known behavioural problems. Initial instruction should concentrate on establishing water confidence. With special needs groups this is particularly important and tests which demonstrate water confidence whilst wearing appropriate equipment are advised.

Canadian canoes The use of open Canadian canoes is becoming more widespread in outdoor education programmes, particularly when the objective of the activity is to emphasise the importance of working together. In addition to strict adherence to

Safety afloat

standard safety principles providers should appreciate that this type of craft is not generally suitable for sea use or white water conditions.

Canoe surfing Canoe surfing is a popular and exciting activity for beginners as well as experts. Leaders should be aware of local characteristics of beach and tide and arrange supervision and beach support appropriate to the skill and experience of the party and the prevailing conditions. Clear limits should be placed on surfing areas in order to maintain control and avoid interference with other people. Sharp pointed kayaks can be hazardous when out of control and should not be used.

Sailing Sailing is a long-established component of outdoor education, providing satisfaction from the handling of a small craft or from contributing to the effective functioning of a large vessel. As an activity it offers opportunities to develop physical skills, as well as the skills involved in planning, thinking and communicating. It can be used to provide experience in decision-making and leadership and to emphasise the importance of teamwork. It can enhance the development of self-confidence and self-reliance, and can help to stimulate an immediate awareness of and respect for the environment.

The importance of confidence when in and on the water needs to be reiterated particularly for dinghy sailors who may be required to work in the water wearing sailing clothing and personal buoyancy in order to rectify a capsize. The ability of sailors to swim prescribed distances is of less significance than their general confidence in water, given that they are urged to remain with the boat in the event of a capsize.

Preparation As with all activities in outdoor education the value of planning and preparation should be emphasised. Local knowledge is again invaluable, particularly in coastal waters, and providers are urged to encourage leaders and instructors to obtain local advice when visiting unfamiliar areas. Venues for sailing should be chosen for their appropriateness to the level of skill and the aims of the activities. Access arrangements will also need to be checked, particularly on inland waters where local arrangements will apply.

Sailing expeditions using small boats must be meticulously planned, undertaken in suitable and well-equipped craft and carried out by appropriately experienced young people. It should be recognised that more skill and stamina are required for extended expeditions. Local sources of information, where possible, should be consulted in order to eliminate unnecessary risks. Voyage plans should be prepared and followed. Any enforced changes should be relayed by providers to local contacts such as coastguards as soon as possible. Preparatory training to cope with potential hazards is essential for all participants and should be regarded as a necessary part of the outdoor education curriculum.

Equipment and clothing Providers and instructors should ensure that all participants are dressed correctly for the activity and that waterproof clothing of sizes appropriate for the

Sailing

participants is available. The example set by the instructor is important. Dry clothing should be readily available ashore. Only wellingtons designed specifically for sailing should be worn afloat. Instructors and crew should wear lifejackets or personal buoyancy aids when afloat. The choice between a full lifejacket and a buoyancy aid should be made by the leader. This will depend on the nature of the activity and the craft in which it is taking place. Buoyancy aids may provide a more practical and safer alternative to lifejackets when low-boomed or single-handed dinghies are being used.

Craft Providers should ensure that all craft are appropriate for the purpose envisaged and are equipped to meet emergencies. The checking of this equipment and acquiring the ability to use it should be regarded as an integral part of the learning experience of all participants. It is essential that the boats used are so designed and equipped that they will float and support the crew after a capsize and that water can be baled out. Providers are recommended to carry out regular checks and tests on the buoyancy of craft.

Leaders Co-ordinators are encouraged to ensure that leaders and instructors are suitably qualified for the proposed level of activity and hold current certificates in the national coaching scheme which is administered by the Royal Yachting Association (RYA). When sailing in coastal waters is planned, co-ordinators should require instructional staff to hold the appropriate RYA tidal endorsement. It is the responsibility of providers to ensure that the ratio of instructors to participants is in keeping with the ability and experience of the group, the type of craft being used and the conditions to be encountered. Co-ordinators are recommended to familiarise themselves with the guidelines contained in the RYA National Proficiency Scheme and to ensure that these are observed by leaders.

Communications An essential feature of the management of any outdoor activity is an effective communication system. At venues selected for sailing a simple, unambiguous communication system is necessary for issuing general instructions, particularly in the event of unexpected changes in the weather. All participants should appreciate, for example, the importance of immediately observing any recall signal. In the interests of group safety the sailing area should be well-defined, known to all concerned and strictly adhered to.

Safety boat An appropriately equipped safety boat, and those qualified to operate it, must be present when sailing is taking place. The staff involved will require skills, experience and judgement if unnecessary intervention is to be resisted with the aim of fostering self-reliance. Care must be taken to select a safety boat with the capability of performing a wide range of functions, particularly if the craft is to be used to accompany sailing expeditions. Detailed advice is available from the RYA.

Cruising Coastal cruising places particular demands on participants in terms of skill, fitness and social relationships. The leader, therefore, must be aware of the nature of

Safety afloat

problems likely to be encountered and have the necessary experience to deal with them during the cruise. The vessel chosen must be appropriate for the task and within the competence of the participants. Off-shore cruising in ocean-going craft is a serious undertaking requiring qualified and experienced staff. Providers contemplating this activity should consider engaging the services of one of the sail training agencies. The guidance contained within the current Department of Transport regulations for sailing and vessels, and current RYA publications on cruising and off-shore sailing should be observed by co-ordinators.

Windsurfing For many participants windsurfing provides excellent opportunities for adventure. The physical skills of co-ordination and balance are extensively developed by the activity. A continuous scheme of learning is essential if progress is to be ensured, as are the right conditions and appropriate equipment.

Precautions Whilst an onshore simulator represents a valuable learning resource for the participant, considerable care needs to be exercised when this equipment is in use. Simulators should be low and stable and meet RYA standards. Supervising staff should possess the RYA Windsurfing Instructor's Certificate; assistant staff should be working towards this qualification. At the initial stages staffing ratios need to be low. Thereafter they will be dictated by the conditions and the experience of the group. Approved personal buoyancy aids should be worn at all times and the supervising leader must ensure that the equipment is appropriate for the type of water and for the skill level of the participants. A suitable safety boat should be present when learners are on the water; in tidal conditions this should be manned by two people. Local knowledge and advice should be sought in order to increase awareness of prevailing conditions. Particular attention should be paid to the onset of exhaustion or hypothermia in participants.

Self-rescue An introduction to self-rescue techniques early in the learning process is important. Participants should also be made aware of the dangers of off-shore winds in tidal and coastal areas. Providers are urged to establish clearly defined windsurfing sailing areas and to institute clear and easily understood signalling systems.

Surfing Surfing is now being incorporated in some programmes of outdoor education. The activity requires the same vigilance as other water-based activities. The British Surfing Association's National Coaching Accreditation Scheme provides courses for instructors who should be qualified in life-saving and first aid. A staffing ratio of 1:6 is recommended. Teaching locations appropriate to the ability of the participants should be selected and the content of the lesson planned accordingly.

When beginners are being introduced to the activity, participants should be paired with a shore-based member who is responsible for observing the member afloat. Management of the surfing zone is critical and participants should be carefully briefed on the necessity of adhering to the incoming and outgoing lane system. A lifeguard watch should be operated whilst the activity is in progress.

Providers are encouraged to ensure that boards selected for beginners have adequate flotation and are suitable for the varying physiques and levels of fitness of the participants. Beginners should wear wetsuits, preferably ones which cover both arms and legs.

Rafting Rafting, either as a task-centred learning exercise or as practice in paddling inflatables on white water rivers, is increasing in popularity. Co-ordinators should be aware of the particular and local hazards associated with these variations of the activity. Leaders should have previous experience of the activity and ideally be qualified in the BCU coaching scheme which covers many of the skills involved.

Sub-aqua Underwater exploration provides a challenging recreational activity. Often young
activities people begin their interest by being introduced to snorkelling in safe conditions. As with all water-related activities, there are basic safety requirements to be followed and a wide variety of equipment available from which to choose. Advice and help are available through the nationally recognised governing bodies of the sport. All equipment should be of good quality and, where appropriate, comply with the current British Standards Institute (BSI) specifications.

Participation in sub-aqua activities should be restricted to those who have completed or have undertaken a recognised course of training. Organisations such as the British Sub-Aqua Club, the Scottish Sub-Aqua Club and the Northern Ireland Federation of Sub-Aqua Clubs should be consulted regarding the local availability of training. There are recommendations about the age of participants and the depth of dives which should be carefully observed. Instructors must be satisfied that participants are physically fit. There are a number of medical conditions such as epilepsy or diabetes which disqualify a person from the sport. Also, those suffering from colds, infection or fatigue should be excluded from the activity until they have recovered. Supervision should be provided on open-water dives, and the use of a safety boat is necessary when diving at sea. Rescue and emergency procedures should be known and practised before participants are introduced to open-water diving.

Given the increased use of dry suits and large-capacity aqualungs, providers must be especially vigilant about the possibility of decompression accidents. When visiting new diving sites, it is recommended that local groups are consulted about the existence of hazards. Additional care must be taken when diving in remote areas such as the west coast of Scotland and this is to be undertaken only by the most experienced participants in the sport.

Rowing Detailed advice and information on rowing can be obtained from the Amateur Rowing Association, but this section reminds co-ordinators of outdoor education

Safety afloat

programmes of matters to consider when rowing-boats are used. The age an physical condition of participants are important factors, and young people shoul not undertake activities and use craft for which they are not properly preparec Where rowing is part of an outdoor education programme then appropriat personal buoyancy may be necessary in some circumstances.

It is the responsibility of the leader to ensure that the conditions are appropriate the equipment is suitable for the participants and someone has been put i charge of the boat. Before being allowed on to the water, participants need to b briefed about local navigation rules and the effects of currents, weirs, sluices an winds. Consideration for others should also be emphasised and some indicatio given of the rights and customs of other water-users. Emergency procedures i the event of a capsize or other accident while rowing should be clearly known b all participants. All providers are urged to draw up appropriate safety guideline for leaders and instructors.

Angling and fishing
These activities are sometimes included within a broad programme of outdoc education, and can be undertaken on a group or individual basis. It is important t emphasise safe practice. The activities should aim to develop environmenta awareness, highlight conservation issues and promote respect for the othe water-users. The seasonal nature of certain aspects of the activity should als be stressed and participants made aware of the importance of observin seasonal limitations.

Regardless of the location of the activity, whether it is a river or canal bank, a lak or loch-side, the sea-shore, or fishing from a boat, a number of safet principles are applicable. Leaders and instructors should be proficient in life saving and resuscitation techniques and aware of the dangers of hypothermia The introduction to first aid should include clear instructions on how to remov fish hooks from flesh.

Personal clothing and equipment appropriate to the environment should b insisted upon. Safety glasses and a hat for protection are important pieces c personal equipment for participants being introduced to fly fishing.

Hazards
Those in charge must appreciate the potential dangers arising from th individualised nature of the activity. Before allowing participants to fish alone o the bank or the shore, leaders must be satisfied as to the expertise and sel reliance of the participants. Where unsupervised activity is likely, parents c guardians should have agreed in writing. Participants should be made aware c potential hazards such as crumbling banks, tides of varying height and speec mudflats, shingle banks, unexpected large waves, and slippery, weed-strew rocks. The dangers of wading in fast and unfamiliar water needs particula emphasis. Sources of local information should be consulted about hazards likel to be encountered.

42

Co-ordinators are urged to consult the appropriate national bodies for information and advice and to participate in the National Anglers Council Proficiency Scheme (NACPS). Providers should review the qualifications of instructors to bring them into line with the Instructors Grade AII level of NACPS.

Bank and shore fishing Whenever possible the leader in charge of bank and shore fishing should be an experienced angler familiar with the local water and with safe access routes. Given the particular problems of supervising the development of young people in this activity staffing ratios in the region of 1:10 should apply. Where appropriate, studded or felt-soled waders should be worn. Instruction in recovery techniques from deep, fast water when wearing waders and in the use of a wading stick should be included in the safety syllabus. When fishing from rocks, lifejackets should be worn and participants need to be alert to the possibility of large waves. A rescue rope or line-throwing buoy should be available.

Fishing from boats Fishing from boats requires particular expertise in boat-handling. Where the activity is undertaken at sea, local knowledge of tides and weather conditions is particularly important. Solo fishing from boats should not normally be permitted. In most cases it is advisable to engage the services of a professional boatman. Any craft that is hired should conform to the requirements laid down by the Department of Transport. Co-ordinators should be aware of the need to use craft which are adequate for the activity and large enough for the numbers taking part. The ratio of staff to the number of young people will be dependent on the type of vessel used. The recommendations of the Department of Transport currently in force should be followed.

Particular attention should be paid to the clothing of participants in sea-going fishing expeditions to ensure that it is warm, as well as wind- and water-proof. Fluorescent coloured clothing which makes accident victims more visible is of particular benefit. Personal buoyancy should be worn. Emergency rations should be carried and the craft checked for the necessary spare and emergency equipment. Above all, co-ordinators need to be satisfied that participants have a level of water confidence in emergency situations appropriate to the environment or area to be visited. It is wise, also, to consider the need to take measures to prevent seasickness.

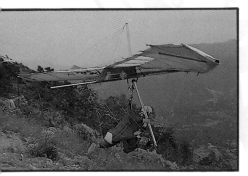

SAFETY

IN THE AIR

Safety in the air

Introduction This section sets out safety precautions which apply generally to airborne activities, including gliding, flying and parachuting. Many activities are specialise and therefore it is recommended that the advice of experts is sought beforehand.

The number of groups flying to destinations abroad has increased in recent years Safety concerns in these situations are more usually dealt with collectively by the national regulatory authorities, the airline company, the local authority, the schoc and the parents, and are not covered here. (A checklist for **safety in the air** is given in Appendix 8.)

Organisation The careful and detailed planning of any airborne activity is of paramour importance. Before an aircraft flight the leader of the party should give to the operator of the aircraft the fullest information about the purpose of the exercis so that the pilot can be briefed on the educational nature of the activity and o the requirements of the party. The captain of the aircraft will, with the background information, be able to brief the party on what to expect during the exercise. At the same time he will be able to issue instructions on matters such a movement about the aircraft, access to the flight deck and general conduct and discipline during the flight. Anyone proposing to take a party of young c inexperienced people on a flight of any kind should make certain that the operator of the aircraft holds relevant, nationally recognised licences c certificates.

Consent The written consent of parents of participants under 18 years of age should be obtained in all instances. National bodies recommend minimum ages for the different airborne activities. The risks inherent in these activities can be minimised by rigid adherence to the code of behaviour produced by the nationa body and by ensuring that only instructors licensed by that body are employed i training participants. The need for a strict code of discipline and adherence to the regulations should be emphasised.

Ground safety Safety on the ground is as important as that in the air. The leader of the grou should be familiar with local safety regulations and see that they are carried ou In the case of an aeroplane flight the strictest discipline is demanded of the grou when walking between the terminal building and aircraft. Generally, and certainl with large groups, this movement should be under the direct supervision of the staff of the aircraft operator. All clothing, exercise books, maps and papers shoul be made secure in case engine slipstream is encountered. The retrieving of an object blown away must be done with the utmost care by a member of staff. O the field, young people should keep a lookout for approaching aircraft; the landin approach of a glider, for instance, may not be heard.

APPENDICES

APPENDIX 1
Draft application form for the approval of educational visits and journeys

(First check whether the responsible authority has its own form.)

This application form, when completed by the leader or co-ordinator, woul provide information to the head or provider which is essential before deciding c approval. *Not all sections will be relevant to every proposed visit or journey.*

School/organisation: ....

Application for approval of journeys and visits

This form should be completed by the leader or co-ordinator in charge of proposed visit and submitted to the provider for approval at the earliest possibl time. When approval is given, one copy should be retained by the provider an another by the leader in charge. Any subsequent changes in plannin organisation, staffing, etc, should be communicated to the provider for approva If required, the provider should seek approval from the responsible authority.

1. Purpose of the proposed visit and specific educational objectives.
   ....
   ....
   ....

2. Places to be visited.
   ....
   ....
   ....

3. Dates and times:
   leaving.. returning.................................
   time .... time ....

4. Transport arrangements. Include the name of the transport company.
   ....
   ....
   ....

5. Name of organising company/agency (if any).
   ....
   ....
   ....

6. Proposed financial arrangements.

....

....

....

NOTE: No financial or other commitments should be made before approval is obtained.

7. Insurance arrangements for *all* members of the proposed party, including voluntary helpers. Include the name of the insurance company.

....

....

....

8. Accommodation to be used:
   Name: ....
   Address: ....
   Telephone No: ....
   Name of head of centre (if available): ....

9. Details of the proposed travel arrangements and programme of activities. Include the name of the travel company.

....

....

....

10. Details of any hazardous activity and the associated planning, organisation and staffing.

....

....

....

11. Names, relevant experience and qualifications and specific responsibilities of *staff* accompanying the party.

....

....

Give the name of the party leader.

....

Appendix 1

12. Names, relevant qualifications and specific responsibilities of other *adul* accompanying the party.

   ....

   ....

   ....

13. Name, address and telephone number of the contact person in the home are who holds all information about the visit or journey.

   ....

   ....

   ....

14. Existing knowledge of places to be visited and whether a preliminary visit intended.

   ....

   ....

   ....

15. Size and composition of the group.

   Age range ....
   Number of boys .... Number of girls..............................
   Adult/pupil ratio..
   Leader/participant ratio ....

16. Parental consent.

   Forms completed/not completed.

   Please attach copy of information sheet sent to parents and the parental conse form.

17. Names of persons with special needs or disabilities or those requiri medication.

   ....

   `.` ....

   ....

   Arrangements for these members of the group ....

To the head/provider
I request your approval for the proposed visit, full details of which are outlined above.
Signed: ....
Leader/co-ordinator

Date: ....

This section to be completed by the head/provider
1. I have studied this application and am completely satisfied with all aspects including the planning, organisation and staffing.
   Approval is given.
2. To the leader/co-ordinator:
   a. Please ensure that I have all relevant information including a final list of members and a detailed itinerary at least seven days before the party is due to leave.
   b. Your report and evaluation of the visit including details of any incidents should be with me as soon as possible but no later than 14 days after the party returns.

Signed: ....
Date: ....

A copy of the completed application form and details of any subsequent changes should be retained by the head/provider.
A copy should also be available for the responsible authority, such as the LEA or the governing body.

APPENDIX 2
Draft parental consent form

(First check whether the responsible authority has its own consent form. Conse may not be required for young people beyond school age.)

School/organisation: ....

1. Details of journey

    Journey/visit to: ....
    From: .... Date/time To:....................................Date/tim

    I agree to my son/daughter .... (nam
    taking part in the above-mentioned visit and, having read the information shee
    agree to his/her participation in any or all of the activities described.
    acknowledge the need for obedience and responsible behaviour on his/her part.

2. Medical Information
    a. Does your son/daughter suffer from any conditions requiring medic
        treatment, including medication?
        If YES, please give brief details.
        ....
        ....
        ....

    b. To the best of your knowledge, has your son/daughter been in contact wi
        any contagious or infectious diseases or suffered from anything in the last fo
        weeks that may be or become contagious or infectious.
        If YES, please give brief details.
        ....
        ....
        ....

    c. Is your son/daughter allergic to any medication?
        If YES, please specify.
        ....
        ....

    d. Has your son/daughter received a tetanus injection in the last five years?
        YES/NO
    Please outline any special dietary requirements of your child.

    I undertake to inform the co-ordinator/head as soon as possible of any change
    the medical circumstances between the date signed and the commencement
    the journey.

3. Declaration
   I agree to my son/daughter receiving emergency medical treatment, including anaesthetic, as considered necessary by the medical authorities present. I understand the extent and limitations of the insurance cover provided.

   I may be contacted by telephoning the following numbers:
   Work: ....
   Home: ....

   My home address is: ....
   ....
   ....

   If not available at above, please contact:
   Name: ....

   Telephone number: ....

   Address: ....
   ....
   ....

   Name, address and telephone number of family doctor:
   ....
   ....
   ....

   Date: .... Signed: ....

   This form or a copy must be taken by the leader on the activity. During holidays a copy should be retained by the responsible authority.

APPENDIX 3
Emergency procedures

In spite of good planning and organisation there may be accidents ar
emergencies which require an on-the-spot response by the leaders. Very few fat
accidents have occurred on educational visits, journeys and expeditions, b
leaders should be prepared for this or other emergencies. The following outlir
guidance is provided for leaders.

*Control and
supervision of the
group*

Share the problem; advise all other group staff that the accident/emergen
procedure is in operation.

Make sure ALL members of the group are accounted for.

If there are injuries, immediately establish the names of the injured people ar
the extent of their injuries.

Ensure that the injured are accompanied to hospital (preferably by an adult th
know).

Ensure that the rest of the group are adequately supervised and have understoo
what has happened and the implications for the rest of the programme.

*Control of
information and
communication*

Restrict access to telephones until you have made contact with the co-ordinato
head, provider or emergency contact point.

News travels very quickly. Immediately make contact with the head, provider
emergency contact point. Give details of the accident or emergency.

The head or provider should alert the chief officer who is responsible for exterr
relations with the press.

The responsible authority may be asked for comment or to give direct assistan
(e.g. payment for overnight accommodation).

Contact with relatives should be made by the head or provider. Ensure th
relatives are informed before the media.

A designated person should act as the ongoing point of contact with the medi
This will involve close liaison with the chief officer.

There should be liaison by the designated person with police and releva
emergency services about what information may be released to the media.

If comment at the scene of the accident or emergency is requested by the mec
enquiries should be addressed to the designated person. The names
participants injured should NOT be released. Caution is required in t
preparation of any statement as legal proceedings may follow an accident (e.
against a coach company, travel operator, hotel, etc.).

Appendix 3

You should prepare a written report for the responsible authority of the accident or emergency at the earliest opportunity and while events are readily recalled. Note the names, addresses and telephone numbers of any independent witnesses.

The Health and Safety at Work Act has implications regarding the reporting of accidents (see p.4). You should be familiar with the current regulations.

Welfare of members of the group and their families
In the event of an accident, young people will need help in coping with shock or trauma. This will also apply to leaders, families and other members of the party.

APPENDIX 4
Checklist for fire precautions and evacuatio procedures

All premises with fire certificates should have fire routine notices. Read them members of your group and make sure they are understood.

Obtain advice from the management on the means of escape available from th premises, including standing camps, and investigate ALL means of escape ensure that they are adequate and unobstructed and, if there are locked door that they can be readily opened from inside.

Always familiarise yourself and those in your charge with the alternative escap routes by physically checking them. A fire drill should be conducted as soon a possible after arrival. Identify the assembly point and ensure the whole party familiar with its location.

Check on fire alarm call point positions. Ensure that each member of the grou knows where the nearest call point is located in relation to his/her room, ar arrange for the alarm system to be tested so that the members of the group ca recognise the alarm. If your room is too far from other members of the group from an escape staircase or escape route, insist on being moved or chang made.

Outline of procedure in event of fire   In the event of an outbreak of fire on the premises, you should give priority to th evacuation of persons in your group and on checking that all are accounted for.

Do not use the lift.

On operation of the fire alarm systems all members of the group should procee in a calm and orderly manner to the prearranged assembly point.

If it is safe to do so, you should check that those in your group have heard th alarm and are evacuating the premises.

Check that all persons are accounted for by carrying out the full roll call as soo as possible at the assembly point.

If any members of the group are found to be missing on roll call, report the immediately and without fail to the fire officer in charge at the scene.

On no account should you or any member of your group re-enter the premises locate or attempt to rescue missing persons after carrying out the procedu above.

Special precautions against fire are necessary at standing camps, particula during periods of dry, hot weather. Procedures need to be established abo conduct in the event of a fire.

APPENDIX 5
Checklist for the conduct of outdoor education activities

ims and objectives

Are you aware of the policies of the responsible authority and sources of advice?

Do you have a written statement of aims for outdoor education and residential experience?

Are the staff involved in outdoor education and residential experiences aware of these aims?

Have the purposes of the visit, journey or activity been agreed with senior management? Are the purposes compatible with the overall aims? Have they also been discussed and shared with the young people, parents, advisers, school governors and the staff of outdoor and residential centres?

Have the purposes been translated into achievable objectives?

Is there a person responsible for co-ordinating outdoor and residential education in the school, college or organisation?

Does the outdoor education programme offer variety and progression?

Is adequate time and attention devoted to preparation, review and follow-up?

Is the level of risk acceptably low? If there is risk, is it integral to the experience or an unnecessary extra?

Have the organisation and the centre identified criteria by which progress in the work may be evaluated?

How is evaluation conducted?

Learning

Has the institution identified what skills, knowledge, and attitudes young people may acquire through outdoor education?

Is the range and quality of the experiences offered sufficient for young people to achieve these objectives?

What are the intended outcomes of these learning processes:
>   in better understanding of environments;
>   in technical competence;
>   in personal and social skills;
>   in social and environmental awareness?

Do experiences meet the needs of all levels of ability?

Are outdoor education programmes designed for young people with different degrees of intellectual, physical, sensory and emotional development?

Appendix 5

Do young people and leaders evaluate their own performance?

Are young people given an opportunity to become actively involved in aspects the planning, preparation, organisation, recording and reviewing of learni experiences in outdoor and residential situations?

Communication and liaison

Do you fully understand the requirements of the responsible authority?

Does the authority offer advisory support and does it have a procedure for vetti the suitability of proposed expeditions?

Do you understand the legal position, particularly in respect of personal liability?

Before a residential visit is made, have the procedures of the authority for t approval of such visits been followed and has there been full consultation w parents?

Have parents given written consent for visits, including those which exte beyond the school day, for emergency medical treatment and for participation the programme of activities?

Do centres foster relationships with the local community? Do they have a pol for contributing to the local community?

Resources (finance, equipment and locations)

Have you made an assessment of what can be achieved within existi resources?

Is there a programme for improving resources?

Before excursions are made to more distant locations, have you giv consideration to the use of suitable local resources?

Are the natural resources of particular locations used with discrimination?

Is due care taken to avoid over-using certain habitats?

Have you given consideration to the resources and services offered by support agencies?

In-service training

Does the organisation encourage leaders to take an interest in experient learning out-of-doors?

Are young leaders assigned to experienced mentors so that techni competence and other aspects of leadership may be acquired gradually und supervision?

Is there a stated policy and programme for staff development and in-serv training in outdoor education?

Are leaders given information concerning how, where and within what time sc they may acquire necessary certification?

APPENDIX 6
Checklist for safety on land

Leaders should consider this checklist in the light of the nature of the area to be visited, the need for specific skills or training and the purpose of the venture. For some school trips, day journeys and field activities with an experienced leader, some of the questions will not apply. Organisers should refer to the publication *Out and About*, listed in Appendix 11.

The group　When operating outside your direct control on self-reliant journeys, can members of the group use a map and compass with confidence in all the conditions likely to be encountered?

Has a route card been prepared giving escape routes, bad weather alternatives and estimated time of arrival?

Is at least one member of the group familiar with local conditions?

Have local and general weather forecasts been studied?

When mountain walking, are the procedures for group movement on narrow ridges and steep and broken slopes well known to the group?

If snow and ice conditions are likely to be experienced are all members equipped with ice axes and crampons and are they trained to use them?

Is the personal equipment of each member of the group suitable for the terrain and for the weather conditions likely to be met?

Has the camping and group equipment been checked and are members knowledgeable and skilful in its use under difficult conditions?

Are tent groups experienced in campcraft and cooking skills? Are they familiar with the planning and preparation of hot meals under difficult weather conditions?

Are the members of the group conversant with accident procedures and have they been given routine and essential information in case of emergency?

The leader　Do your knowledge, skill and experience comply with nationally accepted standards or with locally determined requirements for leadership?

Do you know the individuals in the group well enough to forecast their reactions under trying and physically demanding conditions likely to be met?

Are you competent in providing first aid?

Do you carry the additional equipment recognised as being essential to the safe conduct of the party?

General　Are the nature, purpose and aim of the expedition clearly understood by all concerned?

Appendix 6

Have the parents been informed and have they provided written consent?

Are parents aware of the activities involved?

Does the responsible authority's insurance adequately cover the expedition activities and, if not, has extended cover been taken out?

Has the insurance of voluntary helpers been considered?

Has the expedition been cleared with landowners or official departments?

Is the party familiar with the relevant country and fieldwork codes?

APPENDIX 7
Checklist for safety afloat

For providers and operating authorities

Does your knowledge, skill and experience comply with nationally accepted standards or with locally determined requirements for leadership?

Are standing orders available to regulate water activities and to take account of local conditions and knowledge?

Is personal buoyancy always worn, and does it conform to current BSI/ SBBNF or national governing body specifications?

Are escort boats adequately powered and equipped for the waters and conditions in which they operate?

Have member organisations joined local or national sailing or canoeing associations?

Is insurance cover adequate for all those involved, and is the person in charge of activities aware of relevant conditions in the policy?

Are activities regularly monitored and evaluated?

For leaders directly responsible for activities afloat

a Has the temperature of the water in which the young people may find themselves been considered?

b Does the water temperature influence the instructions given about the disposition of craft and escort boat, and about the clothing to be worn?

c Is there evidence that the young people are confident in the water?

d Are you able to carry out expired-air resuscitation?

e Do young people and staff wear appropriate personal buoyancy when afloat? Are checks made that they are correctly worn?

f Are lifejackets and buoyancy aids regularly tested for air-tightness and wear?

g Is capsize drill understood before young people go out without an instructor?

h Does the person in charge of each craft report that a check of boat equipment and accessories has been completed satisfactorily before departing?

i Is the control of activities managed efficiently?

j Are there readily available records of the young people involved, their programme of activities, the limits imposed, and the stated time for return?

k Are weather forecasts, sailing and canoeing limits, and tidal information obtained before setting out?

l When appropriate, is HM Coastguard informed of the proposed activities?

Appendix 7

M Is there a visual and/or aural recall signal which can be clearly seen or heard by craft at any position in the activity area, whatever the wind conditions?

N Are all young people and instructors aware of the emergency procedures?

O Are participants aware of the National Water Safety Signs devised by RoSPA National Water Safety Committee?

This checklist does not cover the additional requirements for extended inland passages, coastal work or cruises.

APPENDIX 8
Checklist for safety in the air

This checklist offers guidelines for consideration before undertaking various airborne activities.

Have parents been informed of the kind of activities in which participants will be involved and have they given their written permission?

Has the insurance position been checked with the responsible authority?

Do all participants understand the need for strict adherence to the rules and regulations governing the activity?

Are participants appropriately clad for the activity?

Are the centre, equipment and instructors approved by the national body?

Has the policy on the age of participants been adhered to?

Have the educational purpose of the activity and the risks involved been fully explained to the participants and to their parents?

Has a weather report been obtained?

Further advice on airborne activities is available from organisations listed in Appendix 11.

APPENDIX 9
Equipment for expeditions

Items normally worn
or carried for
mountain walking

Boots
Socks
Warm trousers or tracksuit bottoms
Shirts
Sweaters
Underwear
Waterproof jacket/cagoule and trousers*
Gloves*
Woollen headgear*
Gaiters*

*Worn as required according to conditions and weather.

Items for summer
camping
expeditions

1. *Personal*
Rucksack
Sleeping bag and inner
Complete change of clothing
Toilet requisites
Mug, deep plate and cutlery
Plastic sheeting
Whistle
Map
Compass
Torch and spare battery
Matches
Plimsolls/trainers

2. *Group (shared)*
Tent (groundsheet)
Flysheets and poles
Stove
Fuel bottle
Nesting billies
Water bucket
Tin opener
Rations and containers
Washing up (pads, cloths)
Toilet paper
Trowel
Emergency rations
Simple first aid kit

3. *Leader*
Group first aid kit
30–35 m of 9 mm nylon rope (if the terrain makes it necessary)
Spare fuel
Emergency rations
Man-sized poly-bag

Additional items for
winter mountain
expeditions

1. *Personal*
Ice axe*
Crampons*
Overmitts
Sweaters ⎫
Underclothes ⎬ additional
⎭
Scarf
Balaclava
Goggles

2. *Group*
Group-sized nylon tent-sac

3. *Leader*
Emergency flare kit
Deadman belay
Snow shovel

* The use of the ice axe and crampons requires training and a knowledge of safety precautions.

APPENDIX 10
National parks, national nature reserves and regional parks

There are no national parks in Scotland or Northern Ireland but many of the accessible areas are covered by a countryside ranger service able to offer assistance and advice.

Area	Contact
ENGLAND	
Broads Authority	Broads Authority Safety Officer Broads Authority Thomas Harvey House 18 Colegate NORWICH Norfolk NR3 1BQ
Dartmoor	Education Ranger Dartmoor National Park Office Parke Haytor Road BOVEY TRACEY Devon TQ13 9JQ
Exmoor	Youth and Schools Officer Exmoor National Park Exmoor House DULVERTON Somerset TA22 9HL
Lake District	Youth and Schools Liaison Officer National Park Visitor Centre Brockhole WINDERMERE Cumbria LA23 1LJ
Northumberland	Youth and Schools Liaison Officer Northumberland National Park Eastburn South Park HEXHAM Northumberland NE46 1BS

Area	Contact
North York Moors	Youth and Schools Liaison Officer The Moors Centre Danby WHITBY North Yorkshire YO21 2NB
Peak District	Youth and Schools Liaison Officer Peak National Park Centre Losehill Hall CASTLETON Derbyshire S30 2WB
Yorkshire Dales	Education Officer Yorkshire Dales National Park Colvend Hebden Road GRASSINGTON Near Skipton North Yorkshire BD23 5LB

WALES

Area	Contact
Brecon Beacons	Education Officer Brecon Beacons National Park 7 Glamorgan Street BRECON Powys LD3 7DP
Pembrokeshire	Youth and Schools Liaison Officer Pembrokeshire Coast National Park County Offices HAVERFORDWEST Dyfed SA61 1QZ
Snowdonia	Youth and Schools Liaison Officer Snowdonia National Park Information Service PENRHYNDEUDRAETH Gwynedd LL48 6LS
SCOTLAND	Scottish Countryside Rangers Association c/o Lochore Meadows Country Park Crosshill LOCHGELLY Fife KY5 8BA

Appendix 10

Area	**Contact** Nature Conservancy Council Scottish Headquarters 12 Hope Terrace EDINBURGH EH9 2AR
	Countryside Commission for Scotland Battleby Redgorton PERTH PH1 3EW
Fife Regional Park	Fife Regional HQ Fife House North Street GLENROTHES Fife KY7 5LT
Pentland Hills Regional Park	Lothian Regional HQ George IV Bridge EDINBURGH EH1 1UQ
Loch Lomond Regional Park	Strathclyde Regional HQ Strathclyde House 20 India Street GLASGOW G2 4PF
NORTHERN IRELAND	Information Officer Department of the Environment Countryside and Wildlife Branch Calvert House 23 Calvert Place BELFAST BT1 1FY
	Education and Public Relations Officer Department of Agriculture Forest Service Dundonald House Upper Newtownards Road DUNDONALD Co Down BT4 3SB

APPENDIX 11
Some useful publications and addresses

Local education authorities in England and Wales, education departments in Scotland and the education and library boards in Northern Ireland provide information, guidance and details on the safety regulations in outdoor education which apply to schools, colleges and institutions within their responsibility. Contact the local office for further information.

National youth organisations provide information and advice to individual members and groups on the planning of visits and activities. For up-to-date addresses contact National Youth Bureau, 17–23 Albion Street, Leicester LE1 6GD.

Governing bodies provide information and advice on safety matters in their particular sports and activities. Details of relevant publications and leaflets are available from the governing bodies and schools' associations whose up-to-date addresses can be obtained from:

Sports Council, 16 Upper Woburn Place, London WC1H 0QP.

Central Council of Physical Recreation, Francis House, Francis Street, London SW1P 1DE.

Scottish Sports Council, Caledonia House, 1 Redheughs Rigg, South Gyle, Edinburgh EH12 9DQ.

Sports Council for Wales, National Sports Centre, Sophia Gardens, Cardiff CF1 9SW.

Sports Council for Northern Ireland, House of Sport, Upper Malone Road, Belfast BT9 5LA.

Books and leaflets

General

Assistant Masters and Mistresses Association (1987) *Out of School* (3rd edition), London: AMMA.

Association of Heads of Outdoor Education Centres, National Association for Outdoor Education, National Association of Field Studies Officers, Outdoor Education Advisers' Panel, Scottish Advisers' Panel (1988) *Outdoor Education, Safety and Good Practice: Guidelines for Guidelines,* published by Duke of Edinburgh's Award Office, 5 Prince of Wales Terrace, Kensington, London W8 5PG.

Berkshire County Council (1989) *Report of the Altwood School Enquiry Panel,* Royal County of Berkshire.

British Association of Advisers and Lecturers in Physical Education (1989) *Safe Practice in Physical Education* (revised edition), BAALPE, Nelson House, 3–6 The Beacon, Exmouth, Devon.

British Mountaineering Council/Sports Council (1988) *Development, Design and Management of Climbing Walls.*

Buckinghamshire County Council (1985) *School Visit to Cornwall by Stoke Poges County Middle School, May 1985,* Report of Chief Education Officer (Garrett Report), Buckinghamshire County Council.

Appendix 11

Carter, F. (1987) *Educational Visits and Journeys*, National Foundation f« Educational Research for Education Management Information Exchange.

Central Bureau of Educational Visits and Exchanges (1988) *School Travel ar Exchange*.

Central Council of Physical Recreation (1987) *Guide to National Governing Boe Coaching Award Schemes*, London: CCPR.

Central Council of Physical Recreation (1988) *Community Sports Leaders Awa Scheme* (BETA), London: CCPR.

Department of Education and Science (1983) *Learning Out-of-Doors: An HI Survey of Outdoor Education and Short-stay Residential Experience*, Londo HMSO.

Department of Education and Science (1978) *Safety in Physical Educatie* (revised edition 1986) London: HMSO.

Department of Education and Science (1989) *Environmental Education from 5 16*, HMI Curriculum Matters Series, No.13, London: HMSO.

Duke of Edinburgh's Award Expedition Guide (1987).

Duke of Edinburgh's Award (1988) *A Challenge to the Individual: The scheme ar people with special needs.*

Expedition Leaders' Manual, Expedition Advisory Centre, Royal Geographic Society, Kensington Gore, London SW7 2AR.

Hannam, P. (1987) *Simply Safe: Guidelines on Basic Health and Safety at Woi* Bristol: Youth Education Service Publications.

Journal of Adventure Education (quarterly), National Association for Outdo Education.

Lowe, C. (1988) *The School Travel Organiser's Handbook 1989*, Hobso Publishing PLC, Bateman Street, Cambridge CB2 1LZ.

Mortlock, C. (1984) *The Adventure Alternative*, Cicerone Press, 2 Police Squar Milnthorpe, Cumbria LA7 7PY.

National Association of Head Teachers (July 1988) *Council Memorandum « Supervision*, London: NAHT.

National Union of Teachers (1986) *Beyond the Classroom: Guidance from t National Union of Teachers on School Visits and Journeys*, London: NUT.

Nature Conservancy Council (1982) *Wildlife, the Law and You*, Peterboroug Nature Conservancy Council.

Professional Association of Teachers (1987) *Safety on School Journeys.*

School Curriculum Development Committee (1987) *Out and About: A Teache Guide to Safe Practice Out of School*, London: Methuen.

Youth Hostels Association (1989) *'DATAPACK' for Teachers and Leaders.*

Road safety Assistant Masters and Mistresses Association (September 1986) *The School Minibus and the Law*, London: AMMA.

Department of Transport (1987) *Highway Code*, London: HMSO.

Dring, T. and Collins, M. (1986) *An Introduction to Basic Minibus Driving*. Birmingham: RoSPA.

Royal Society for the Prevention of Accidents, Safety Education Department, road safety education materials, Birmingham: RoSPA.

Medical Department of Education and Science (1987) *AIDS – Some Questions and Answers: Facts for Teachers, Lecturers and Youth Workers*, London: HMSO.

Department of Education and Science (1986) *Children at School and Problems Related to AIDS*, London: HMSO.

Department of Health and Social Security, *Medical Treatment during Visits Abroad*, Leaflet SA30, *Notice to Travellers – Health Protection*, Leaflet SA35. London: HMSO.

Molloy, C.C. (for St John Ambulance) (1987) *Essentials of First Aid*, Reading: Hills & Lacey.

St John Ambulance, St Andrew's Ambulance Association and the British Red Cross Society (1987) *First Aid Manual: Emergency Procedures for Everyone at Home, at Work or at Leisure*, London: Dorling Kindersley.

Special needs British Epilepsy Association (1988) *Epilepsy: A Guide for Teachers*, Leeds: British Epilepsy Association.

Croucher, N. (1981) *Outdoor Pursuits for Disabled People* (2nd edition), London: Disabled Living Foundation.

Thompson, N. (ed.) (1984) *Sports and Recreation Provision for Disabled People*, London: Architectural Press, for Disabled Living Foundation.

Addresses Association of Heads of Outdoor Education Centres, D. Shearman, Aberglaslyn Hall, Beddgelert, Gwynedd LL55 4YF.

British Red Cross Society, 9 Grosvenor Crescent, London SW1X 7EJ.

British Safety Council, 62 Chancellors Road, London W6 9RS.

Central Bureau of Educational Visits and Exchanges, Seymour House, Seymour Mews, London W1H 9PE.

Child Accident Prevention Trust, 75 Portland Place, London W6 9RS.

Council for Environmental Education, School of Education, University of Reading, London Road, Reading RG1 5AQ.

Development Training Advisory Group, 2 Fern Grove, Welwyn Garden City, Herts AL8 7ND.

The Duke of Edinburgh's Award, 5 Prince of Wales Terrace, Kensington, London W8 5PG.

Appendix 11

Expedition Advisory Centre, Royal Geographical Society, Kensington Gore, London SW7 2AR.

Fire Protection Association, 140 Aldersgate Street, London EC1A 4HX.

Health and Safety Commission, Baynards House, 1 Chepstow Place, Westbourne Grove, London W2 4TF.

Health Education Authority, Hamilton House, Mabledon Place, London WC1H 9TX.

Mountaineering Council for Scotland, Caledonia House, 1 Redheughs Rigg, South Gyle, Edinburgh EH12 9DQ.

National Association for Environmental Education, West Midlands College of Higher Education, Gorway, Walsall, West Midlands WS1 3BD.

National Association for Outdoor Education, 50 Highview Avenue, Grays, Essex RM17 6RU.

National Association for Outdoor Education (Scotland), 57 Melville Street, Edinburgh EH3 7HL.

National Coaching Foundation, 4 College Close, Beckett Park, Leeds LS6 3QH.

National Trust for Scotland, 5 Charlotte Square, Edinburgh EH2 4DU.

National Youth Bureau, 17–23 Albion Street, Leicester LE1 6GD.

Outdoor Education Advisers' Panel, M. Styles, Education Department, Springfield, Maidstone, Kent ME14 2JL.

Paul Vander-Molen Resources Centre for Disabled Exploration, The Model Farm House, Church End, Hendon NW4 4JS.

Physical Education Association of Great Britain and Northern Ireland, 162 Kings Cross Road, London WC1X 9DH.

Royal Society for the Prevention of Accidents (RoSPA), Cannon House, The Priory Queensway, Birmingham B4 6BS.

St Andrew's Ambulance Association, 48 Milton Street, Glasgow G4 0HR.

St John Ambulance, 1 Grosvenor Crescent, London SW1X 7EF.

School and Group Travel Association, 2 Meadowside Road, Cheam, Surrey SM2 7PF.

School Journey Association, 48 Cavendish Road, Clapham South, London SW12 0DG.

Scottish Panel of Advisers in Outdoor Education, Secretary, Hill Park Education Centre, Ben View, Bannockburn FE7 0JY.

Scottish Physical Education Association, 1 Preston Field Court, Saline, Dunfermline, Fife KY12 9UU.

Scottish Youth Hostels Association, General Secretary, 7 Glebe Street, Stirling FK8 2JA.

Young Explorers Trust, Royal Geographical Society, Kensington Gore, London SW7 2AR.

Youth Hostels Association, Trevelyan House, 8 St Stephens Hill, St Albans, Herts. AL1 2DV.

Safety on land

Books and leaflets

Mountaineering

Barry, J. and Jepson, T. (1987) *Safety on Mountains* (2nd edition), Manchester: British Mountaineering Council.

Blackshaw, Alan, *Mountaineering*, Penguin. (To be revised in two volumes, 1990.)

British Mountaineering Council (1988) *Mountain Code*, Manchester: British Mountaineering Council.

British Mountaineering Council (1988) *Mountain Hypothermia*, Manchester: British Mountaineering Council.

Langmuir, E. (1984) *Mountaincraft and Leadership*, Manchester: Mountainwalking Leader Training Board, and Scottish Sports Council.

Loxham, Jim, *Climb When Ready*, Edgeley, Manchester.

Mountaineering Council of Scotland, *Going to the Hills. The Scottish Mountains Code.*

Other

Aerial Runway Code. Available from The Scout Association Training Department. Gilwell Park, Chingford, Essex E4 7QW.

Alpine and Nordic Ski Technique and Instruction Manuals, British Association of Ski Instructors.

Duke of Edinburgh's Award, *Land Navigation: Route Finding with Map and Compass*, Wally Keay, April 1989.

McNeill, C., Ramsden, J. and Renfrew, T. (1987) *Teaching Orienteering: A Handbook for Teachers, Instructors and Coaches*, Colchester: Harveys, in conjunction with the British Orienteering Federation.

Addresses

Basic Expedition Training Award, Central Council of Physical Recreation, Francis House, Francis Street, London SW1P 1DE.

British Association of Ski Instructors, Grampian Road, Aviemore, Inverness-shire PH22 1RL.

British Cycling Federation, 36 Rockingham Road, Kettering, Northants NN16 8HE.

British Horse Society, British Equestrian Centre, Stoneleigh, Kenilworth, Warwickshire CV8 2LR.

British Mountaineering Council, Crawford House, Precinct Centre, Booth Street East, Manchester M13 9RZ.

British Orienteering Federation, Riversdale, Dale Road North, Darley Dale, Matlock, Derbyshire DE2 2HX.

British Ski Federation, Brocades House, Pyrford Road, West Byfleet, Surrey KT14 6RA.

English Ski Council, Area Library Building, The Precinct, Halesowen, West Midlands B63 4AJ.

Appendix 11

Mountain Leader Training Board (Northern Ireland), Sports Council for Northern Ireland, House of Sport, Upper Malone Road, Belfast BT9 5LA.

Mountain Leader Training Board for Wales, c/o Department of Zoology, University College of Wales, Aberystwyth, Dyfed SY23 3DA.

Mountainwalking Leader Training Board, Crawford House, Precinct Centre, Booth Street East, Manchester M13 9RZ.

Ramblers Association, 1–5 Wandsworth Road, London SW8 2XX.

Scottish Mountain Leader Training Board, Caledonia House, 1 Redheughs Rigg, South Gyle, Edinburgh EH12 9DQ.

Scottish National Ski Council, Caledonia House, 1 Redheughs Rigg, South Gyle, Edinburgh EH12 9DQ.

Field studies

Books and leaflets   Council for Environmental Education and National Association of Field Studies Officers in co-operation with Field Studies Council and the Nature Conservancy Council: *The Outdoor Studies Code.*

Countryside Commission, *The Country Code.*

Geographical Association (1987) *Geography Outside the Classroom: Guidelines for the conduct of fieldwork.*

Institute of Biology (1983) *Safety in Biological Fieldwork.*

Jones, E. and Rogers, S. (1989) *Exploration Seashore: A beginner's guide to active exploration of the seashore*, Marine Conservation Society.

National Association of Environmental Education (revised 1988) *Organisation Outdoor Studies and Visits.*

Nature Conservancy Council (1982) *Wildlife, the Law and You*, Peterborough Nature Conservancy Council.

Sidaway, R. (1988) *Sport, Recreation and Nature Conservation*, Sports Council.

Addresses   Council for Environmental Education, School of Education, University of Reading, London Road, Reading RG1 5AQ.

Countryside Commission, John Dower House, Crescent Place, Cheltenham, Gloucestershire GL50 3RA.

Countryside Commission for Scotland, Battleby, Redgorton, Perth PH1 3EW.

Environmental Education Council, Department of Environmental Science, University of Stirling, Stirling FK9 4LA.

Field Studies Council, Information Office, Preston Montford, Montford Bridge, Shrewsbury SY4 1HW.

Geographical Association, 343 Fulwood Road, Sheffield SIO 3BP.

Marine Conservation Society, 9 Gloucester Road, Ross-on-Wye, Hereford and Worcs HR9 5BU.

National Association of Field Studies Officers. Secretary: P. Greenough, Arnfield Tower Field Study Centre, Manchester Road, Tintwistle, Hyde, Cheshire SK14 7NE.

National Trust, 36 Queen Anne's Gate, London SW1H 9AS.

Nature Conservancy Council, Northminster House, Peterborough PE1 1UA.

Scottish Field Studies Association, Nairn Estates Office, Priory Lodge, Victoria Road, Kircaldy KY1 2QU.

Woodland Trust, Autumn Park, Dysart Road, Grantham, Lincs NG31 6LL.

Safety afloat

Books and leaflets

General

Central Council for Physical Recreation (1988) *The Water Sports Code*, London: CCPR.

Edwards, L. (1985) *Inland Waterways of Great Britain* (6th edition, revised and enlarged), Huntingdon: Imray, Laurie Norie & Wilson.

Good, G.C. (ed) (1983) *Canoeing Handbook*, Weybridge: British Canoe Union.

Hazzard, J. (1982) *Instructors' Training Handbook,* London: British Sub-Aqua Club.

HM Coastguard, *Boardsailing Safety Guide, Coastguards: The Coordinators, Small Craft Safety Checklist, Yacht and Boat Safety Scheme*, London: HMSO.

Marine Conservation Society, *Underwater Conservation Code*, leaflet and slides, Ross-on-Wye: Marine Conservation Society.

Royal Life Saving Society in conjunction with the Leeds Permanent Building Society (1984) *The Blue Code for Water Safety*, London: The Royal Life Saving Society.

Royal Society for the Prevention of Accidents, Water and Leisure Safety Department (1985) *Be Water Wise Code;* (1986) *Water Wise Awareness Pack*, Birmingham: RoSPA.

Royal Yachting Association (1983) *National Certificate Scheme: Syllabus and Logbook,* Eastleigh: Royal Yachting Association.

Medical and special needs

British Epilepsy Assocation (1987) *Swimming and Epilepsy,* Leeds: British Epilepsy Association.

British Sports Association for the Disabled (1983) *Water Sports for the Disabled*, London: A.& C. Black.

Addresses

Amateur Rowing Association, 6 Lower Mall, Hammersmith, London W6 9DL.

Amateur Swimming Association, Harold Fern House, Derby Square, Loughborough LE11 0AJ.

Beach Safety Advisory Committee, Dunworth House, Donhead St Mary, Shaftesbury, Dorset SP7 9DG.

British Canoe Union, Mapperley Hall, Lucknow Avenue, Nottingham NG3 5FA.

British Sub-Aqua Club, 16 Upper Woburn Place, London WC1H OQW.

Appendix 11

British Waterways Board, Melbury House, Melbury Terrace, London NW1 6JY.

HM Coastguard, Department of Transport, Room 8/1, Sunley House, Hig Holborn, London WC1V 6LP.

Royal Life Saving Society, Mountbatten House, Studley, Warwickshire B80 7NN.

Royal Yachting Association, RYA House, Romsey Road, Eastleigh, Hampshir S05 4YA.

Scottish Canoe Association, Caledonia House, 1 Redheughs Rigg, South Gyl Edinburgh EH12 9DQ.

Water and Leisure Safety Department, Royal Society for the Prevention Accidents, Cannon House, The Priory, Queensway, Birmingham B4 6BS.

Welsh Canoeing Association, Pen-y-Bont, Corwen, Clwyd LL21 0EL.

Safety in the air
Information on relevant safety procedures and regulations can be obtained fro the following organisations:

Air Education and Recreation Organisation: Mr I. R. Simpson, (Personal – AERO), Area Education Office, 14 A/B North Street, Guildford, Surrey GU1 4AS.

British Association of Parascending Clubs, 18 Talbot Lane, Leicester LE1 4LR.

British Gliding Association, Kimberley House, 47 Vaughan Way, Leicester LE1 4SG.

British Hang Gliding Association, Cranfield Airfield, Cranfield, Bedfordshire MK43 0Y

British Parachute Association Ltd, 5 Wharf Way, Glen Parva, Leicester LE2 9TF.

Civil Aviation Authority (Airworthiness Division), Sipson House, 595 Sipson Roa Sipson, West Drayton, Middx UB7 0JD.

Government departments
Department of Health, Richmond House, 79 Whitehall, London SW1A 2NS. Te 01-210 3000.

Department of the Environment, 2 Marsham Street, London SW1P 3EB. Tel. 0 276 3000.

Department of Transport, 2 Marsham Street, London SW1P 3EB. Tel. 01-27 3000.

HMSO publications on behalf of the Department of Education and Scienc appear in Sectional List 2, available free from HMSO.